THE WORLD'S
GREATEST
CROOKS &
CONMEN

THE WORLD'S GREATEST CROOKS & CONMEN

NIGEL BLUNDELL

HAMLYN

First published in hardback in 1982
by Octopus Books Limited

This edition first published in 1991 by
The Hamlyn Publishing Group Limited
part of Reed International Books
Michelin House, 81 Fulham Road
London SW3 6RB

ISBN 0 600 57227 7

Printed in Great Britain at the Bath Press, Avon

Contents

Acknowledgements

For contributions, criticism and constructive advice, the author would like to thank the following: Roger Boar, Robin Corry, Terry Hasler, David Williams, Marian Davidson, Rob Robbins, David Nicholson, Sonia Roberts, Geoff Barker, Jeremy Beadle, Clive Doig, Ann Mayhew and Stella Duggan.

Introduction

THE DEVIL, they say, has all the best tunes. He also has some of the best stories.

Like it or not, the rascals, scoundrels and rogues of this world are generally more interesting characters than the good guys. In fact, as well as fiction, their names and their escapades are often better remembered than those of the heroes.

To prove it, we have gathered together in this volume a remarkable array of men and women whose deeds, although never laudable, nevertheless make compelling reading.

They're not all malicious, hardened criminals, of course, some of the characters in this book are even rather lovable.

You may not approve of them. . . . But you can't help admiring them!

Chapter One

Thieves and Villains

'Crimes, like virtues, are their own rewards'
George Farquhar

How the great escaper became a runaway success

A handsome, weatherbeaten man of 52 strode out to greet waiting crowds in Bridgetown, Barbados. His reception was tumultuous. In the carnival atmosphere of cheering and singing, he announced exultantly 'Champagne for everyone – the drinks are on me!'

Yet the hero of the moment was no popular republican, no victorious sportsman. He was a crook – and not a very good one at that. His name: Ronald Biggs.

In 1963, eighteen years earlier, a gang of thieves held up a mail train at a remote spot in the English countryside and got away with £2½ million in used banknotes. The daring robbery was labelled the crime of the century.

Best-known of the so-called Great Train Robbers was Ronnie Biggs. Not because he was one of the gang leaders – his part in the raid was relatively minor – but because of his amazing ability, after later escaping from jail, to keep one step ahead of the law.

Every night used banknotes were sent from Scotland by rail to London to be destroyed. The money travelled in a special coach which formed part of the regular night mail train from Glasgow to Euston. The amount varied but always rose dramatically after a Bank Holiday. On August 3, the gang believed, it might be as much as £4 million.

The gang were a colourful bunch. Principal among them were: Bruce Reynolds, aged 30, fond of the 'good life', who considered himself a cut above London's East End criminal fraternity; Gordon Goody, a 32-year-old tough loner with a sharp taste in clothes and girls; Ronald 'Buster' Edwards, aged 30, club-owner, and devoted family man; Charlie Wilson, 32, a resourceful criminal friend of Reynolds; Jimmy White, a quiet 42-year-old ex-paratrooper; Bob Welch, 32 a South London club owner; Tommy Wisbey, a 32-year-old bookmaker; and Jim Hussey, aged 30, who ran a Soho restaurant.

The gang also brought in three specialists: 'wheels' man Roy James, 23, a silversmith and racing driver; Roger Cordrey, a 38-year-old florist who was an expert at 'adjusting' railway signalling equipment; plus a retired train driver.

At the last minute, they also recruited a small-time thief and decorator, with a pretty wife, engaging smile and a yearning for the luxury life he could never afford. His name was Ronald Biggs.

Bridego Bridge in Buckinghamshire was the lonely spot where the gang decided to rob the train. Their base was isolated Leatherslade Farm, 26 miles away.

At around midnight of August 2, these motley 'soldiers' of fortune, dressed in an assortment of commando gear, set out from the farm for Bridego Bridge with two Land-Rovers and a lorry.

Cordrey switched on two warning lights – one several hundred yards up the track, another closer to the bridge. The first would cause the train to slow, the second would bring it to a halt. The gang also cut the lines to trackside emergency telephones and to nearby farms and cottages.

Aboard the train at precisely 3 am, driver Jack Mills looked out for the usual green trackside light. But tonight it was amber. He put on the brakes and throttled back the mighty diesel. The overhead signal gantry came into sight. It glowed red. Mills stopped the train and asked his fireman, David Whitby, to use the emergency telephone beside the gantry to find out what was going on.

Whitby vanished into the darkness. Mills heard him ask someone: 'What's up, mate?' Then nothing. In fact, Whitby had run into Buster Edwards. Bundled down the embankment, he was pinioned to the ground.

Back in the cab of the train, driver Mills was being attacked from both sides. He was overpowered from behind and hit twice across the head.

The engine and two front coaches, including the one carrying the money, were separated from the train and were moved the short distance to the bridge by the ex-driver. The gang then smashed the doors and windows of the High Value Packages Coach with an axe and crowbars. Five Post Office guards were made to lie on the floor while the gang unloaded 120 mailbags along a human chain which led down the embankment and into the back of the lorry.

Then, sweating but jubilant, they drove back in their convoy to Leatherslade Farm. All had gone according to plan, but for the blow on the head received by driver Mills. It proved to be a big 'but' – for that moment of violence weighed heavily against the robbers at their trial.

But, for the time being, the future looked rosy. The gang spent the rest of the night counting out the money, setting aside sums for major bribes and backhanders, and sharing out the rest. In all, there was £2½ million.

Having concocted their alibis and arranged to salt away their shares until the

---

Bold front

A beautiful girl toured the big stores in Denver, Colorado, and made dozens of purchases – but only from male assistants. The girl paid for the goods with a credit card which she offered, still warm, from her bikini top. The girl got away with at least $1,000 of goods before anyone bothered to check whether her credit card was genuine.

hue and cry was over, they went their separate ways, brimming with confidence. It was short-lived . . .

Damning evidence had been left behind – fingerprints, clothing and vehicles. Although the robbers had arranged for an associate to stay at the farm and clean it from top to bottom, the job was never done. The contract was bungled.

Detectives had no difficulty in identifying the men from fingerprints and palm prints. A Monopoly board was a mine of information to forensic scientists. Soon the faces of the robbers were on 'wanted' posters all over Britain.

Within a year, most were in jail. The sentences meted out for 'a crime against society' shook the thieves – and created public sympathy. Goody, Welch, James, Wisbey and Hussey all got 30 years, although they were eventually released after serving 12. Wilson and Biggs also got a 30-year term. Cordrey was given 14 years and freed after seven. But some of the robbers were to give the police enormous trouble in the years to come.

White evaded arrest for three years before being captured in 1965, and was jailed for 18 years, of which he served nine.

Reynolds and Edwards hid out in London for almost a year, then fled to Mexico City. They spent money at a frightening rate and both eventually returned to Britain.

In 1966 Edwards surrendered. He was given a 15-year sentence and served nine. Reynolds was arrested in 1968 and received 25 years. He was released in 1978.

In prison the train robbers were kept under the closest security because two of them had made sensational escapes . . .

In 1965 Wilson escaped from Winson Green Prison, Birmingham, and joined Reynolds and Edwards in Mexico City. But he too tired of the place and moved to a smart home near Montreal, where he was caught in 1968. He returned to continue his 30-year sentence and was freed 10 years later.

The second escape was even more sensational – and launched a criminal legend. In July 1965 Ronald Biggs was 'sprung' from London's Wandsworth Prison by a daring group of associates. He scaled the wall and landed on the roof of a waiting furniture van.

After undergoing plastic surgery in France to restyle his nose and cheek-bones, Biggs collected some of his share of the loot and flew to Australia. He set up home in a Melbourne suburb, took a job as a carpenter and was joined by his wife Charmian and their three sons. There they lived under assumed names for several years, with only one event to mar their happiness – the death in a car crash of their eldest son.

Eventually Biggs received a tip-off that Scotland Yard detectives were on to him and that he was in imminent danger of arrest. This time he fled to Brazil.

Life without his family was difficult. He settled near Rio de Janeiro and

Ronald Biggs relaxing on a beach near his home in Rio de Janeiro

sought solace in drugs, alcohol and women.

Early in 1974 a reporter of a London newspaper tracked him down and set about writing his story. But the paper's executives tipped of Scotland Yard about their projected scoop. On February 1, 1974, Chief Superintendent Jack Slipper and another police officer arrived in Rio to arrest Biggs. To their dismay they learned that Brazil had no extradition agreement with Britain. The Rio police refused to hand him over.

Then Biggs's young Brazilian girl-friend, Raimunda, announced that she was pregnant. It was news which left the lucky father-to-be overjoyed – simply because the father of any Brazilian child could not be deported.

So Biggs went free again. And Slipper, after his much-publicized swoop, flew home alone.

It was not till 1981 that the great escaper found himself back in prison, not thanks to Scotland Yard, but to a gang of kidnappers.

Masterminding the kidnap plot was a 36-year-old ex-British Army sergeant named John Miller. He and his four-man team arrived in Rio in April and befriended the unsuspecting Biggs, long separated from Raimunda but living with six-year-old son Mike. One night, outside a Copacabana bar, the gang overpowered him, gagged him and stuffed him inside a sack, which they bundled into a waiting van.

Biggs was smuggled out of the country through the northern port of Belem, put aboard a chartered yacht and taken outside Brazilian territorial waters.

The kidnappers and their hostage sailed north to the Caribbean where, in an extraordinary auction, the hapless Biggs was held to ransom.

Ringleader Miller based himself at a Barbados hotel and told the assembled representatives of the press that he would 'sell' Biggs to the highest bidder.

But now the operation went wrong. The yacht on which Biggs was held broke down and, as it drifted into Barbados waters it was seized by coastguards. The kidnappers quietly dispersed and Biggs was thrown into prison to await extradition to Britain.

As Biggs languished in a cockroach-infested cell in Bridgetown, Barbados, hope must almost have gone. Extradition was surely only a formality. But it proved otherwise.

Biggs's closest friends in Rio were Cockney John Pickston and his Brazilian wife Lia. They hired top lawyer Ezra Alleyne to fight the extradition. After three weeks of legal wrangling, the island's Chief Justice, Sir William Douglas, ruled that the extradition treaty between Barbados and Britain was not valid.

Biggs walked free – with £30,000 for the costs of his case.

The crowds outside the court swept him through the streets in an impromptu display of Caribbean dancing. The delighted Biggs shouted: 'Isn't it bloody marvellous? I just don't believe it. Champagne for everyone.

Even more emotional was Biggs's return to Brazil. At Rio airport the tough train robber was reduced to tears as he was reunited with son Mike.

They clung to one another as Biggs said: 'I didn't know if I would ever see you again.' He gave the boy a table tennis game he had spent the last of his money on. And little Mike gave his father an Easter egg and twenty pictures he had painted – all inscribed 'Welcome home Daddy.'

Then the tired ex-train robber was handed a brand-new Brazilian passport, an amazing gesture by the adopted country where he had become a national hero. He waved the passport above his head and vowed: 'This marks a new chapter in my life. I am now able officially to work for a living. I'm going to get a job . . . anything honest!'

The underground 'mole' behind the world's biggest bank robbery

The 1976 raid on the Nice branch of the Société-Générale was the biggest bank robbery ever. Afterwards, owners of rifled strongboxes put in claims totalling £6 million, but French police believe the haul could have been nearer £50 million.

Most of the raiders, who tunnelled from a sewer into the bank's vaults, were never caught. The mastermind, Albert Spaggiari, was arrested but escaped from a courtroom and was believed to have headed for South America. To the French, he became something of a cult hero. He even wrote a book about the robbery, which was made into a film.

Spaggiari evidently set his heart on big-time crime in his teens. At 16 he applied in writing to join a group of Sicilian bandits, but received no reply. Two years later he joined the army and served as a paratrooper in Indo-China, where he had three citations for bravery in action. But after staging a robbery at a nightclub he was court-martialled, jailed and dishonourably discharged.

He then joined the OAS and went to Algeria. The OAS hated France's President, General de Gaulle, and Spaggiari claimed to have organized an assassination attempt – along the lines of the one featured in Frederick Forsyth's thriller, *Day of The Jackal*. When de Gaulle visited Nice, Spaggiari had him in the sights of a rifle from the upper window of his mother's shop. The reason he did not fire was that his OAS chief failed to give the order.

A year later Spaggiari was arrested with four accomplices for printing and distributing right-wing pamphlets. Police searching their print shop and homes discovered an illegal cache of arms and ammunition. Because of his previous record, Spaggiari got four years' imprisonment, while his friends were put on probation.

After his release, he became a photographer, opening a shop and specializing in smart weddings and pictures of the rich and famous who pass through Nice.

His work brought him in contact with the town's top people, and he cultivated a friendship with the mayor, Jacques Médecin. Later Médecin became France's Minister of Tourism and took Spaggiari with him on a tour of Japan as his official photographer.

Spaggiari used the profits from his photographic business to invest in a chicken farm in the hills. He lived there with his wife Baudi, his collection of German imperial army spiked helmets and an armoury of guns, ammunition and explosives. It was at the farm that he and his accomplices plotted the biggest bank raid ever.

Spaggiari, lean and handsome and always smoking a big Dom Miguel cigar, was a popular and respected character in Nice.

The city was considered by many to be the crime capital of southern France, having inherited the dubious honour from Marseilles. Violence and gang warfare were a part of everyday life. At stake were the rich pickings from drugs, vice and robberies.

Much of the illicit profit ended up in safe-deposit boxes in bank vaults. Other boxes in the vaults of the Société-Générale would have held assets undeclared for tax reasons. Many victims of Spaggiari's raid claimed much less than they had lost – for fear of attracting the attention of the tax inspectors or the police.

Some of the boxes broken open by the thieves held humble secrets. One was filled with coffee, sugar and biscuits, presumably hoarded in case of the outbreak of World War Three. Others held chocolates, toffees, cigarettes and flasks of alcohol, belonging to secret smokers, drinkers and dieters who could not resist the occasional lapse.

Spaggiari is thought to have got hold of a map of the town's sewer system with the help of a highly placed town hall official. He rented a safe-deposit box at the Société-Générale to note the layout and security system.

To check for electronic sensors, he left a wound-up alarm clock in his box, to see if its ringing set off detectors. It did not. There was no alarm system in the vaults because they were considered impregnable. The walls were 5 ft thick.

Spaggiari decided to tunnel from the nearest sewer to the vaults, then break through the masonry walls with electric drills. After 18 months' planning, the gang entered the sewer system via a small underground river.

They reached the vaults of the Société-Générale by digging a tunnel 24 ft long and 4 ft high. It took them two months, working by night and laboriously carrying their equipment in and out every evening and morning. They carried the soil away in plastic sacks, to dump in the hills above Nice. The tunnel, supported at the correct intervals by jacks, was constructed so professionally that when police discovered it they first checked on ex-miners.

The gang broke through to the vaults on the evening of Friday, July 20, 1976. They brought in an air pump to set up a ventilation system. Then they opened safe-deposit boxes with jemmies, taking notes, gold and jewellery, and scattering share certificates and private documents over the floor.

The gang could have worked undisturbed until the early hours of Monday morning but for one piece of bad luck – rain.

Their getaway sewer was a main storm drain. A heavy downpour threatened to flood it and on Sunday the gang made a hurried escape in rubber dinghies after rifling 317 of the 4,000 deposit boxes in the vaults.

Before leaving, they welded shut the door leading to the bank to give themselves a few more hours before the robbery was discovered. A bank employee who tried the door on Monday morning assumed it was stuck and it was not until lunchtime that a professional was called in to cut through it.

In their haste, Spaggiari and his gang left behind thousands of pounds' worth of equipment. Police found heavy-duty blow torches, 27 gas cylinders, 11 crowbars, pit-props, sledgehammers, jemmies, bolt-cutters, lamps, hacksaws, rope, pliers, hammers, spanners, drills, cooking stoves, eating utensils, empty wine bottles and the remains of meals. On one wall was scrawled the message: 'Without anger, without violence, without hatred'. Above it was the peace symbol.

While bank employees were still trying to free their welded-up vault door, the raiders were counting and sharing their loot, a task which took them from Monday morning until Wednesday evening.

Spaggiari was eventually traced through a shop from which he had bought equipment for the raid – and by the Dom Miguel cigar butts found in the vaults.

On March 10, 1977, Spaggiari was being questioned by an examining magistrate about the disposal of the loot, which he steadfastly claimed to have handed over to an underground OAS-style group. The prisoner complained to the magistrate that the room was stuffy and moved towards a window, apparently for some fresh air. He threw the tall casement open and jumped.

Spaggiari fell 20 ft, landed with an expert paratrooper's roll on a parked car, and sprang on to the pillion of a waiting motorbike. As he sped away, he turned and made a rude gesture to the police. After a 15-minute journey to the airport, he caught the early evening flight to Zurich.

After his escape, sightings were reported in Spain and South America. But it was felt in France that some police were only half-hearted in their efforts to catch the thief whom many regarded as a folk hero.

He escaped to prove his innocence

Alfie Hinds was the Houdini who ran the police ragged in the 1950s when he escaped three times from prison. He broke out each time to protest his innocence of a robbery conviction which landed him 12 years in jail.

Alfie's running battle with the police and the whole legal system began in 1953 when he was convicted of taking part in robbing London's big department store, Maples, of £30,000 in wages.

Alfie, who was born in 1917, had a criminal past. He had been to approved school and Borstal, and during the Second World War had deserted from the army.

But after his marriage in 1947 to Peg Stoodley, a docker's daughter, Alfie went straight. He opened a business dealing in war surplus goods and second-hand cars, and handling demolition work. Peg and Alfie had a son, born in 1948, and a daughter born in 1951.

Throughout his trial at the Old Bailey Alfie protested his innocence. The police claimed he had led a gang which blew open the safe and escaped with the wage money. Alfie said he was at home with Peg when the store was robbed.

But the jury didn't believe him and the judge, Lord Goddard, sentenced Alfie to 12 years preventive detention.

Alfie, describing the trial as a 'farce', was determined to fight back. The campaign to prove his innocence was to involve him in 31 court appearances between the time of the Maples robbery in 1953 and the final hearing in 1965.

His first appeal for a fresh hearing was rejected by the courts. So Alfie decided he must get out to draw the public's attention to his case.

In 1956 he was cooped up in Nottingham Prison, studying law with a driving determination to use every twist and turn of the legal system in his fight for freedom.

His plan was to escape to Eire where he believed he could convince an Irish jury of his innocence.

There were two escape plans then being hatched at Nottingham – one a mass break-out and another involving just one man – a smash and grab driver who was serving eight years.

Alfie said: 'I did not join the mass attempt. My problem was that if I broke prison I was committing a crime. The golden thread which ran through all my years of imprisonment was that I must not commit one crime in order to prove

Alfie Hinds on his way to prison accompanied by a huge police guard

that I was innocent of another.'

He discovered that if he escaped at the same time and by the same route as another prisoner, but provided he had not been involved in any planning, all he could be accused of was 'escape from lawful custody', which was not a criminal offence.

Alfie knew of the one-man escape plan but never let on. When his fellow prisoner made his break, Alfie simply tagged along.

Reunited with Peg, he moved to the Clapham area of London. He bombarded the newspapers with letters explaining the reason for his escape. He even promised to give himself up if he could get an inquiry.

Despite the publicity, no new hearing was promised. So Alfie took the ferry to Ireland. Then he contacted Peg, getting her to send over some money to buy a cottage a few miles south of Dublin.

But in August 1956 it all went wrong. Alfie was arrested as he went to pick up a consignment of tools from a Dublin shipping company.

Back in Pentonville, Alfie spent two years in fruitless legal wrangles trying to prove that he had been unlawfully brought back from Eire and that the Maples case should be reopened. But even as he made a succession of court appearances, a second escape plan was forming in his mind.

Alfie decided to make his getaway during one of his many visits to the Law Courts in London. Each time he arrived, his escorts removed his handcuffs, took him for tea in the staff canteen in the basement and then upstairs to the lavatory before his hearing started.

Alfie arranged with an old friend, due for release from Pentonville Prison, to make a key for the lavatory and leave it taped to the underside of one of the canteen tables.

On the day he planned to escape, Alfie was escorted as usual to the Law Courts. Down in the canteen, his trembling fingers groped beneath the table – and closed round a packet. It was unexpectedly big for a key but he managed to slip it into his pocket without arousing the suspicion of the prison officers.

Warily he undid the package in his pocket. Inside, to his surprise, was a padlock. What was it for?

Tea finished, Alfie and his guards made their way up the stairs to the court and the lavatory. One glance at the door showed Alfie that the plans had changed. 'There', in his own words, 'were two of the biggest and brightest nickel-plated screw-eyes I had ever seen, one on the door itself and the other in the right-hand jam.'

'I assumed my prison friend had been unable to fit the lock and that this was his solution.'

Rushing ahead of his escorts, the padlock gripped firmly in his right hand, Alfie opened the door to the lavatory with his left hand. As they entered, he slammed it shut.

Within a second, the padlock was in place and Alfie was away again, down the stairs and out into the street. There, waiting to take him to London Airport was his brother Bert and a friend, Tony Maffia.

At the airport they found they had missed the Dublin flight. So they drove to Bristol. There, as a result of a circulated description, Bert was mistakenly arrested as the escaper. Alfie, sitting quietly in the airport lounge, was picked up as a suspected accomplice. But at the police station a prison officer arrived and identified the right man. Back went Alfie to Pentonville.

In June 1958 Alfie made his final escape – this time from Chelmsford Prison in Essex. As with his first break-out, he waited until just one man was on his way 'over the wall' – and followed him.

This time his fellow escaper was Londoner Georgie Walkington, serving seven years, who planned to escape from the prison yard with the aid of some keys.

Once outside, both men made a dash for a waiting car and were away before police had time to set up road blocks. They stayed together in a caravan in Kent before going their own ways.

Georgie was caught at a London dog track but Alfie reached Ireland by boat from Liverpool. Using assumed names, he set himself up as a car dealer in Dublin.

Things went well – until Alfie was caught smuggling cars across the border between Northern Ireland and Eire. His fingerprints were sent away for identification and the startled Customs men only then discovered that their smuggler was none other than the king of the escapers.

He was sent to prison for six months in Belfast for smuggling before being returned to Britain in November 1960 to finish his 12-year sentence.

Within a month Alfie was making legal history. An appeal to the House of Lords was finally under consideration. In December he made several visits to the House Appeals Committee – the first time that a prisoner had been permitted to argue in person before the noble peers.

Hoodwinked

A raider put a pillowcase over his head and held up a store in Riverside, California. But after blundering around and knocking into display counters, the bandit got the message that it is always best to cut eye-holes in the mask! He raised a corner of the pillowcase to find his way out of the store, was instantly recognized by a customer, and was later arrested by police.

But again his hopes were dashed. His application for leave to appeal to the Lords was thrown out.

A few days later Alfie was on his way to the top security prison, Parkhurst, on the Isle of Wight.

Then, in 1962, he got his lucky break. Ex-Chief Superintendent Herbert Sparks, who had investigated the Maples robbery, had written a series of articles for a Sunday newspaper. One of them told how he had caught Alfie Hinds. It implied, of course, that Hinds was guilty. In January 1963 Alfie issued a writ for libel against the detective. Just over a year later the case was heard. Alfie spent six days in the witness box.

In his summing up the judge, Mr Justice Edmund Davies, asked the jury: 'Has Hinds spoken with the voice of truth about the Maples robbery, or is he a plausible liar who appears to have attracted to himself in some quarters wholly unmerited sympathy and support?'

After five hours of deliberation the jury found for Alfie and awarded him £1,300 damages.

The following day Alfie heard that the Home Secretary, Henry Brooke, had ordered his immediate release.

Despite his lawyer's advice, Alfie refused to stop battling to completely clear his name. He still insisted on a retrial and in November 1965 his appeal opened at the Court of Criminal Appeal. But it was to be the old disappointments all over again. His appeal was dismissed by the court and later by the House of Lords.

Alfie had won his case with the libel jury but had been unable to get the original conviction against him removed.

He went to live in semi-retirement with Peg in St Helier on the island of Jersey, becoming a do-it-yourself property developer, buying up old properties and renovating them himself.

His keen and agile brain, which had become sharpened through endless hours of battling in the courts, earned him a place in the Channel Islands Mensa Society – an organization for people of super-intelligence.

Warm thanks

A 27-year-old pregnant Swedish girl named Else Haffner won the sympathy of magistrates when she appeared before them on a shoplifting charge. They put her on probation – but their character judgement was soon shown to be faulty. As Else left the court at Malmo, Sweden, she was arrested again . . . and charged with walking out in a fur coat belonging to one of the magistrates.

Ice-cool crooks

Ice-cool nerve seems to be the principal qualification for a life of crime. It was certainly needed in the case of The Great Frozen Asset Robbery.

In 1980, staff at pubs and clubs in Camden, North London, were baffled by the pools of water which appeared under their cigarette machines. They discovered that an ingenious crook had got away with thousands of cigarettes by making ice 'coins' and putting them in the slots. Then he would vanish with his loot while the evidence literally melted and evaporated.

The coolest courage, plus a dash of sheer daring, helped a thief who had been caught red-handed by a woman as he fled from her house carrying a shotgun and the family silver in a plastic bag.

With police patrol cars and a Royal Air Force helicopter on his tail, the fugitive raced away on foot, abandoning his getaway car. Then, on a sudden inspiration, he stopped to seek sanctuary – at a police college.

The brazen bandit knocked on the door of the college at Bramshill, Hampshire, and asked if he could use the phone. He called a cab – and disappeared.

Even more daring were the thieves who stripped the lead from the roof of a police station in Coventry. The building, which the police authority was trying to sell at the time, had to have £5,000 spent on it to make the roof waterproof again.

'If you can lift it, take it' seems to be the motto of the criminal crowd. A banner advertising a crime prevention week in Reading, Berkshire, was stolen. And another thief took the trouble of removing a cardboard cut-out of a Canadian Mountie from a police exhibition at Aylesbury, Buckinghamshire.

A couple who broke into a chemist's shop in Ilkeston, Derbyshire, made a bed from disposable nappies, downed a bottle of energy-giving drink and made love before leaving with goods worth £144.

A gang broke through an elaborate security system to raid the home in Turin, Italy, of a wealthy businessman who earned his fortune making burglar alarms.

After a bigger haul were the three men who boarded an El Salvador Airlines DC-6 jet at Miami airport in 1979. They filed a flight plan for Haiti and took off, stealing the plane. The theft was discovered when the real crew arrived.

One crook who made a clean break was the 23-year-old convict who literally swept out of a Paris jail. He was given a broom and carried on brushing, unnoticed, through the gates and away.

But for sheer cheek, there is no case to beat that of the British bridegroom who invited his boss to the wedding. The bridegroom, a 34-year-old chauffeur, for once did not have to take the wheel, as he and the guests – boss included – were whisked by limousines to the church in Grimsby.

Two of the bridegroom's best friends, however, were not invited to the wedding. They had a prior engagement that very day. For while the bridegroom stood at the altar saying 'I do', his two friends were hard at work – snatching a safe, containing between £15,000 and £20,000, from the boss's home.

The chauffeur, however, did not long enjoy wedded bliss. The conspiracy was uncovered and he was jailed for three years.

The criminal clergy

A dog collar is no deterrent when it comes to fleecing the innocent. The Rev Harry Clapham didn't mind where the cash came from. Even his own flock stumped up to line his pockets, and when he was caught he went to prison for three years.

But the Rev William Dodd, active almost two centuries earlier, who strayed just once and forged the signature of a lord on a bond, paid dearly for his crime – he was executed.

Harry Clapham was the vicar of St Thomas's Church in Lambeth, South London, in the 1930s when he stumbled on the perfect way to rip off the unsuspecting public.

While visiting a patient in hospital, he noticed piles of postal orders and cheques on a desk in an official's office – the result of an appeal for subscriptions to the hospital.

It was like a vision to someone struggling to keep a wife and two children on a vicar's salary of £400 a year, particularly to someone who was as addicted to money as the Rev Clapham.

When he got back to South London he laid his plans to cash in on the public's good nature. Nobody, he thought, would ever suspect a minister of the cloth of pocketing the proceeds of an appeal. And he was right.

He first set about buying a list of people who were well known for their generosity and who usually contributed to charity appeals.

Then he wrote begging letters explaining how desperately his church needed cash for restoration work and to help the poor of the parish. The response amazed even Harry Clapham. Cheques and postal orders poured in as a result of his heart-rending appeals.

His main helper was Constance Owens who worked as his secretary and book-keeper. She was a former schoolteacher who dressed as a nurse and called herself Sister Connie.

Clapham drafted in a small army of volunteers to work in the vestry sending out begging letters as fast as they could stick down the envelopes. It was later estimated that they were issuing up to 200,000 letters a year.

Clapham then played his trump card. He arranged for his brother Willie to move south from their home town of Bradford, Yorkshire, and take over a small sub-post office. Clapham now had a place where he could cash the mounting pile of postal orders and cheques without the risk of someone asking awkward questions.

As the money continued to pour in, so he began to live the life of his dreams. Decked out in expensive hand-made suits, he holidayed in such places as the West Indies and the Holy Land and drove around in expensive foreign cars.

By the late 1930s the Charity Commissioners began to get suspicious of the Rev Clapham. Scotland Yard was called in and, although they found plenty of activity at the church, there was no evidence that the vicar was involved in a massive fraud.

But then Clapham made a fatal mistake. He applied to a charity for assistance. He told them he was a poor clergyman trying to put his son through Cambridge. To qualify for a grant, his income would have had to be less than £400 a year.

This time he was arrested and charged with attempting to obtain money under false pretences.

In June 1942 he was found guilty at the Old Bailey of 21 charges and sent to Parkhurst Prison on the Isle of Wight to serve a three-year sentence.

He was defrocked while in prison but was released early because of ill health. Waiting for him was Sister Connie, his secretary and helper at St Thomas's.

They lived together in a small cottage in the country until he died in 1948. He left her £9,000, but the rest of his ill-gained fortune, estimated at £200,000 – worth about £2 million today – was never recovered.

Barely worth it
Drinkers got a shock when they flocked to a pub in Norfolk, England, which was advertising topless bar staff. The staff were all men.

The Rev William Dodd was a well-known and well-respected public figure in the 18th century. But that didn't save him from the gallows. . . .

Dodd worked hard for many charities and everyone agreed that he was a kind, Christian gentleman. He even had the confidence of the King to whom he was chaplain.

But just before Christmas 1776 Dodd found himself in debt. He didn't owe a lot but his creditors were pressing for payment. So he forged the signature of Lord Chesterfield who lived close by, on a bond for £4,200.

Shortly after the bond was cashed, an investigator who worked for the firm that loaned the money found a discrepancy in the signature. The document was shown to Lord Chesterfield and the game was up.

The firm demanded their money back immediately but Dodd was unable to recover it all and was sent for trial.

Lord Chesterfield refused to help the cleric or even put in a good word for him, despite the fact Dodd had been his teacher and had treated him almost like a son.

Dodd was convicted at the Old Bailey in February 1777 and sentenced to death. Despite a huge public outcry, petitions for mercy and a deputation from the Lord Mayor of London and the Common Council to the King, he was hung at Tyburn.

The politician who faked his own death

Sixty-five-year-old Mrs Helen Fleming was happy to help the pale Englishman who approached her on Miami Beach on a grey, blustery day in November 1973.

Mrs Fleming who ran the Fontainebleau Hotel beach office, had already talked to him some ten days before. He had then told her that he was in Florida on business and that on a previous trip all his possessions had been stolen from the beach. That was why he now asked Mrs Fleming to be good enough to look after his clothes while he went for a swim. The old lady was glad to oblige such a polite, well-spoken gentleman.

The Englishman also impressed on Mrs Fleming his name. He mentioned it several times, and she had no trouble in recalling it later. The name was . . . John Stonehouse.

Stonehouse, 48-year-old Member of Parliament, strolled down the beach to the choppy sea – and vanished. He left behind him a wife, two children, a mistress, a constituency, several ailing companies and debts of about £800,000.

Next morning, James Charlton, a director of one of Stonehouse's companies, who had travelled to Miami with him, reported to the police that his partner had not been seen all night. A search was organized but no body could be found. It was assumed by everyone that he had drowned.

But John Stonehouse had not drowned. His 'death' was simply the final step in an amazingly devious plot.

At the time of his supposed death, Stonehouse was in fact strolling along Miami Beach to a derelict building near the Fontainebleau. There he retrieved a hidden suitcase containing clothes, money, travellers' cheques, credit cards and a passport – all in the name of Joseph Markham. He took a cab to Miami International Airport, boarded a plane to San Francisco and booked into a hotel there under his assumed name.

Over the next week he made his leisurely way by air to Australia. From room 1706 of the Sheraton Hotel, Honolulu, he made two phone calls to his beautiful mistress, Sheila Buckley at a London hotel. He went night-clubbing in Honolulu, sight-seeing in Singapore, and on November 27 flew into Melbourne.

There, in the heat of a southern summer, 'Joseph Markham' lazily acquired a suntan, planned a reunion with his young mistress, and congratulated himself on the success of the most brilliantly executed and foolproof deception of the decade . . . or so he thought.

John Thomson Stonehouse had always been an arrogant man. His conceit made him few friends as he carved a career in politics and business. He wanted to be a millionaire but he ended up in debt. He aimed to be Prime Minister but he ended up in jail.

Stonehouse first entered the House of Commons as a Labour MP in 1957, and subsequently held various ministerial posts, including Postmaster General. But when Labour lost power in 1970 he was offered only a minor post in the shadow cabinet. He turned it down and decided to use his political contacts to enter the business world and 'make a million'.

Financial independence, he told his beautiful wife Barbara, would allow him to return full-time to politics and make an attempt at the Labour leadership. But again his ambitions outstripped his ability.

Stonehouse formed 20 companies in five years, including a merchant bank. One by one they ran into trouble. His little empire only lasted as long as it did because of the way he manipulated funds between one company and another. Whenever the accountants were due to inspect the books of one company, cash would be pumped into it from another so that trading figures looked good.

It was a survival system that could not last. Finally, Stonehouse owed more than £1 million. Banks and credit card companies were demanding £375,000 and he had signed personal guarantees, that he had no chance of honouring, to the tune of £729,000.

By 1974 Stonehouse knew that a Department of Trade investigation was imminent. It would expose him as a liar and a cheat, signal the collapse of his companies, and lead to personal ruin, disgrace – and possibly prosecution for fraud. So he turned to the only ally he could fully trust – his mistress.

Mrs Buckley, 20 years younger than her lover, first worked for Stonehouse as his secretary when he was Minister of State for Technology. With her long black hair, full lips and flashing eyes, the 22-year-old beauty was a popular figure in the Commons. But she had eyes only for her boss. Separated from her husband, in 1973 she moved into a nearby apartment and became Stonehouse's mistress. Her pet name for him was 'Dum Dum'.

After her divorce in 1973, on the grounds of her husband's adultery, Sheila Buckley and her 'Dum Dum' set in motion a plan to salvage as much as possible from what remained of Stonehouse's companies. His eventual aim was to tuck away a nest-egg of more than £100,000 in banks in Switzerland and Australia and use the money to establish himself and his mistress in a new life together with fresh identities in New Zealand.

But first John Stonehouse had to 'die'. . . .

The initial step was to find someone else, someone who was *really* dead, so that he could assume that man's identity. As MP for Walsall, Staffordshire, Stonehouse tricked a local hospital into giving him details of men of his age who had died in the wards. He told them he had money to distribute to widows and that he was carrying out a survey. They gave him two names.

He used the same cover story when he called on Mrs Jean Markham and told her how sorry he was that her 41-year-old husband Joseph had died some weeks earlier of a heart attack.

He extracted from Mrs Markham all the information he needed for his plot to steal her dead husband's identity – particularly the fact that since Mr

---

Thieves in a flap

Cat burglars couldn't believe their eyes when they found a giant 2½ ft dog flap in the back door of a house they were about to rob in Berkshire, southern England. They crawled through, subdued a 4-ft Great Dane called Jasper and fled with £5,000 of jewellery.

Markham had never travelled abroad he had not needed a passport.

Then Stonehouse repeated his act with Mrs Elsie Mildoon, whose husband Donald had also died in the same hospital.

Everything was now ready. Stonehouse obtained copies of the two men's death certificates. Then he applied for a passport in Markham's name. He had himself photographed in open-necked shirt with hair brushed straight back, large spectacles, and a wide grin to distort his features.

He signed copies of the photograph, certifying it to be a true likeness of Joseph Markham, in the name of Neil McBride MP. Stonehouse knew that McBride was fatally ill with cancer. He died two months later.

On August 2, 1974, the Passport Office issued British Passport Number 785965 in the name of Joseph Arthur Markham. Stonehouse had his new identity.

In order to establish Markham as a real person, he got him a private address in a cheap London hotel and a business accommodation address as J. A. Markham, export-import consultant. He opened a bank account as Markham, deposited sums of money in it, then transferred the money to another Markham account with the Bank of New South Wales in London. He flew to Switzerland and put large sums in special Markham accounts there; and he obtained an American Express credit card in the dead man's name.

By November 1973 Stonehouse had no fewer than 27 different accounts in his own name in 17 banks, as well as nine accounts in the names of Markham or Mildoon. The ground plans had been well laid for his disappearance. But there was still one more major test to make.

On November 6 Stonehouse flew to Miami, supposedly to try to raise a big investment to save his ailing merchant bank. On the beach he chatted with Mrs Fleming. He travelled out under the name of Markham, even buying his plane ticket with a Markham credit card. No one was suspicious. The dummy run was a success.

Ten days later he was back in Miami on his final business trip – this time travelling on his own passport – and it was then that he performed his vanishing trick on Miami Beach. A day later the Miami Beach Police Department contacted London with the message: *John Stonehouse presumed dead.*

And 'dead' John Stonehouse might have stayed – but for the most astonishing stroke of bad luck.

The day after his arrival in Australia, Stonehouse called at the Bank of New South Wales in Collins Street, Melbourne. There he checked that Aust. $24,000 had been transferred from London in the name of Markham. He withdrew $21,500 in cash and walked down the road to the Bank of New Zealand, where he introduced himself as Donald Mildoon. He said he was planning to emigrate to New Zealand and wished to deposit $21,500 in cash.

John Stonehouse surrounded by crowds as he leaves Brixton prison

The teller to whom he handed the money was 22-year-old Bryan King. Later, returning from lunch, Mr King spotted Mr Mildoon emerging from the Bank of New South Wales. Mildoon strolled down the street to the Bank of New Zealand. There he deposited another $2,200 in cash.

The young man was suspicious. He told his boss, who telephoned the Bank of New South Wales. 'No,' he was told, 'We have no customer by the name of Mildoon. But we do have a newly arrived British immigrant named Markham who has been drawing out large sums of money in cash.'

The bank notified Victoria State Police and from that moment Stonehouse, alias Markham, alias Mildoon, was watched. The police did not have to wait long for his next move. For the following day Stonehouse boarded a plane at Melbourne Airport and flew to Copenhagen for a secret meeting with Sheila Buckley.

On December 10 he was back in Melbourne. While he was paying a call on his bank, Stonehouse's apartment was visited by Detective Sergeant John Coffey of the Melbourne Fraud Squad. He found nothing incriminating – but a book of matches caught his eye. They came from a hotel which Coffey had once photographed while serving as a steward on a cruise liner almost 20 years earlier. The hotel was the Fontainebleau, Miami Beach.

Coffey had Stonehouse closely tailed 24 hours a day. His actions were entirely unsuspicious. The only regular event in his life was his daily walk to buy *The Times*: but he could never wait until he was home to begin reading it. He always searched through it intently as he stood on a street corner.

Coffey bought copies of the newspaper, trying to discover what the Englishman was looking for. All that he found were reports about the disappearance of another Briton, Lord Lucan, wanted for the murder of his family's nanny.

Coffey naturally assumed that Mr Markham and Lord Lucan were one and the same man. But three days later he read about inquiries into the affairs of another missing Englishman, John Stonehouse MP, who had vanished from the Fontainebleau Hotel, Miami Beach. Coffey remembered the book of matches.

Victoria police called Scotland Yard and asked them urgently to airmail photographs of both Lucan and Stonehouse. The Yard also supplied the information that Stonehouse had a long scar on his right leg.

Early in the morning of Christmas Eve, Coffey and other detectives, armed with revolvers, arrested 'Mr Markham'. At first Stonehouse refused to answer questions. But when his right trouser leg was raised to reveal a scar described by Scotland Yard, he admitted his real identity.

In the fugitive's pocket was a letter addressed to Donald Mildoon. It read: 'Dear Dums, do miss you. So lonely. Shall wait forever for you.' It was from Sheila Buckley – one of many she wrote to Stonehouse while he was on the run.

Nothing to declare

A customs officer was suspicious about a lorry that had just driven off an English Channel ferry at Dover, Kent. He sauntered up to it, knocked on the side and shouted: 'Are you all right in there?' Back came the reply from 22 illegal Asian immigrants: 'Yes!'

On the day of his arrest in Melbourne, Stonehouse telephoned his wife Barbara. Unknown to either of them, the call was recorded. Stonehouse apologized to her, describing what had happened as a 'brainstorm' and explaining that by adopting another identity he hoped to set up a new life.

He concluded with an amazing request. He asked his deserted wife to fly out to Melbourne and to bring his mistress as well. 'Bring Sheila,' he said, 'and we'll link up. If the Australian authorities will allow it, I will remain here and start a new life. . . .'

Stonehouse then spoke to his 14-year-old son, Matthew, telling him that he would understand it all one day and urging him to be brave.

He ended the call with a final plea to his wife to fly to his side with Sheila Buckley in tow: 'Please tell her . . . and try to persuade her. I know she'll need enormous support. The poor girl's been going through hell like you have. I feel for you both.'

Incredibly, wife and mistress flew out separately to join Stonehouse who was by now out on bail. But after an emotional scene, with Stonehouse threatening to commit suicide, Barbara returned home. Sheila Buckley stayed on in Australia with her lover – a sort of phoney honeymoon for them both – until in April 1975 an extradition order was signed. Three months later the couple were flown back to Britain. Finally, in April 1976 their trial began at the Old Bailey.

It cost the British taxpayer an estimated £750,000 to bring John Stonehouse to justice. There was a six-week preliminary court hearing, six barristers involved in the 68-day trial, and a subsequent civil enquiry cost £100,000.

For almost two years an eight-man Scotland Yard fraud team had been tied up sifting through mountains of documents. They had visited America, Australia, Switzerland, Holland, Hawaii and Liechtenstein. Witnesses were brought from Australia and Hong Kong; altogether more than 100 people gave evidence in court.

On August 6, 1976, guilty verdicts to 14 charges involving theft, forgery and fraud rang out in the Old Bailey's historic Number One Court.

Jailing Stonehouse for seven years, the judge, Mr Justice Eveleigh, said: 'You are no ill-fated idealist. In your evidence, you falsely accused people of cant, hypocrisy and humbug – when your defence was all these things.'

Sheila Buckley collapsed in tears as she was given a two-year suspended sentence for helping her lover spin his web of fraud. Throughout his years in prison, she stood by him. He suffered two heart attacks and for several days seemed close to death in a prison hospital. Sheila Buckley visited him regularly.

Stonehouse served only three years of the seven-year sentence. And when he left jail, sick, bankrupt and broken, Sheila and he moved in to a small £13-a-week love-nest in an unfashionable area of London.

In February 1981 the couple married at a secret ceremony in the small Hampshire town of Bishop's Waltham. Perhaps at that ceremony the new Mrs Stonehouse recollected the words she spoke to reporters after her lover's arrest in Australia in 1974 . . . 'If I had the same decisions to make all over again tomorrow, I feel certain that those decisions would remain the same.'

Bandit forgot to remove the cork from his gun!

Irishman Eddie McAlea planned the hold-up of a watchmaker's shop with clockwork precision. He bought a cheap imitation .38 revolver, two reels of caps and a pair of women's tights for a mask.

Outside watchmaker Philip Barrett's shop, Eddie tightened his grip on the revolver and slipped the tights over his head. Then he sprung into action. He burst into the shop shouting 'This is a stick up. Get down!'

But no one moved. For Eddie, 37, had forgotten to take the cork out of the barrel.

When he realized his career as a big-time crook was up, the bungling bandit went out with a bang. As he fled into the street, he ripped off his mask – and Mr Barrett recognized him. For only the day before, Eddie had sold him his own watch.

Eddie was later caught and was hauled up before Liverpool Crown Court, where he was jailed for 30 months after admitting assault with intent to rob and possessing an imitation firearm. The court heard that Eddie, who asked for a psychiatric report on himself, had been released from prison only six days earlier.

Watchmaker Mr Barrett said: 'At first I thought the robbery was the real thing. But when I spotted the cork stuck in the barrel, I knew the fellow must be daft. It's the kind of story Irish jokes are made of.'

Bungling bandits

Plenty of crooks are caught because of their incredible clangers. A gunman who robbed a Paris grocer lost his hat as he ran away. Inside was his name and address, and police were waiting for him when he got home to count his loot.

An Italian bank robber tripped over a doormat when he burst into a Milan bank. As he fell, his mask dropped and his revolver went off. He clambered up, ran towards the cashier but lost his footing again on the slippery floor, grabbing the counter for support and dropping his gun.

As customers and staff began laughing, the robber fled in embarrassment – straight into the arms of a policeman who was writing him a ticket. He had left his car illegally parked.

A bungling bandit in Denver, Colorado, crashed his getaway car into a lamp post but escaped on foot. Back home, however, he was fumbling for his door key when he shot himself in the leg. Police caught up with him clutching his leg with one hand and his loot with the other.

There was trouble in store for a West German shoplifter who shinned down a drainpipe to escape police. He leapt from an 8 ft wall and found himself in the exercise yard of Dusseldorf jail. Warders found six stolen watches in his pocket, and before long he was doing time.

Two British burglars put police in the picture when one of them found a camera in the house they were raiding. For a joke, he took a photograph of his accomplice. But they dropped the camera as they made a quick getaway, and Tyneside detectives returned it to the owner, a 75-year-old woman. Three months later she had the film developed; among the snaps was a picture of a

---

Repentant robber

A bandit walked into a bank in Davenport, Tasmania, put a bag on the counter and ordered the girl teller: 'Fill it up – I've got a gun.'

She put all her loose cash in the bag and when the raider demanded more she got bundles of notes from other tellers. Eventually the robber told her: 'That's enough for me' – and walked out with about £5,000.

Minutes later he reappeared, put the loot back on the counter and told the astonished bank teller: 'Sorry, I didn't really mean to rob you.' Then he waited for the police to arrive.

---

burglar carrying the loot. Police picked up both men within a few hours.

A mugger in Majorca made the mistake of trying to snatch the handbags of two German great-grannies. The women, both 77, tied him up, locked him in the boot of his car and drove him to a police station in Palma. He was taken to hospital suffering from shock.

When a Missouri crook stole a car with a radio-telephone, his number was soon up. Police listened to his calls, and swooped when he arranged a business meeting in Kansas City.

A not-too-bright British bungling burglar had no trouble breaking into an apartment in Chester. It was getting out again that had him foxed. Not even an axe would budge the front door after it jammed shut. The red-faced raider opened a bottle of Scotch as he waited for the owner to turn up and turn him in.

Safebreakers in England's West Midlands were baffled when their oxyacetylene torch failed to cut through a door. It was not hot enough because they had forgotten to turn up the oxygen. After several hours they finally melted a hole large enough to put a hand through. It was not until they had been captured and brought to court that they learned that the door had not even been locked.

Another would-be bandit armed himself with a toy revolver for a raid on a Yorkshire village store that was planned to the last detail. He had his motorcycle parked for a fast getaway and wore his full-face crash helmet as a mask. But he forgot one thing – round the helmet, in inch-high letters, was painted his name! Police had little trouble tracing him.

Chapter
Two

Frauds and Swindlers

'Successful crimes alone are justified'
John Dryden

Evita: the glamour and the greed

Eva Peron was the champion of the poor. They adored her. They lavished their humble devotion upon her with an almost religious fervour. They called her Santa Evita – 'Little Saint Eva'.

In the years following World War Two she was a heroine to Argentina's descamisados – the 'shirtless ones' – whose idolatry made her, for a while, the most powerful woman in the world.

As wife of Argentinian military leader Juan Peron, Eva moved regally among the masses, distributing gifts to the poor. Without warning, she and her retinue would dramatically appear in a peasant village and hand out sweets to the children and food packages to their parents.

The grateful recipients of her largesse wore rags. Eva boasted furs, finery and glittering jewellery. To outside observers, the contrast seemed incongruous. Yet that, Eva always insisted, was how her people wanted it. She was the only glamour in their impoverished existence, she argued, and they needed her.

But that glamour was not just for show. It was many years before the full truth was known, but beautiful Evita and her handsome husband – those two champions of Argentina's poor and oppressed – had spent all their years in power busily lining thier own pockets.

Eva Duarte was the illegitimate child of a poor provincial woman. She was born in 1919 – though she always claimed, with ruthless feminism, that it was 1922. By the time she was 15, she had moved to Buenos Aires with her first lover and was trying to get jobs as an actress.

She was 24 when she met Colonel Juan Peron, who was twice her age. She was then a small-time radio starlet earning £4 a week as a disc-jockey and heroine of the station's soap operas. Peron and the other leaders of Argentina's right-wing military junta arrived at the radio station to appeal for funds for the victims of an earthquake. Colonel Peron, still straight-backed and athletic, was captivated by her deep, seductive voice.

From that moment on, it was Eva who regularly appealed for funds for Peron's Social Services Ministry. In doing so, she built his political charisma. She became his spokeswoman.

'He doesn't care a button for the glittering uniforms and the frock coats,' she purred. 'His only friends are you, the descamisados.'

When the too-powerful Peron was ousted by the junta in 1945, it was Eva who single-handedly regimented the support of the young officers and the

Eva Peron in 1947

workers to reinstate him.

Two years later she married him. And the following year, with Eva at his side, Juan Peron was swept into the presidential palace on the shoulders of the descamisados and with the backing of the powerful unions.

As wife of the president, Eva Peron's ambitions and her past became even more starkly conflicting. She dripped with diamonds, wrapped herself in mink.

When she was snubbed by the genteel, aristocratic ladies who ran the nation's charities, Eva sacked them all and launched the Eva Peron Social Aid Fund. She ordered dresses from France and directed second-hand clothes to the farms and shanty towns. Children were showered with toys. The people were mesmerized. They worshipped her.

Juan Peron's power was based on the trade unions, Eva's on the descamisados. Their regime seemed unassailable. But when Eva sickened with incurable cancer Juan Peron faced the loss of his popular 'voice'.

Eva grew thin and shrunken. At those few political functions she attended, she had to be physically supported by her husband. She complained: 'I am too little for so much pain.'

On July 26, 1952, at 8.25 pm, Eva Peron died. She was 33. Almost on her last breath, her body was rushed away to be embalmed by an eminent pathologist who had been standing by for weeks. He operated on her emaciated body, replacing her blood with alcohol and then with glycerine, which kept the organs intact and made the skin almost translucent.

The nation went into an orgy of mourning. Two million people filed past her coffin. Seven were killed in the crush. There were plans to build memorials to her throughout Argentina. Most of them got no further than the drawing board. For in 1955 a period of roaring inflation led to Peron's overthrow.

The deposed president fled to Spain, where he remained in exile for 20 years. Meanwhile, his successor, General Lonardi, made every effort utterly to discredit the Perons.

He opened the Perons' homes to the public. On display were 15 custom-built sports cars, 250 motor scooters, the safes where Peron kept his $10 million in 'ready cash'. Much, much more had been salted away abroad.

Also revealed were Juan Peron's secret Buenos Aires love nests – apartments lined with furs and mirrors where 50-year-old Peron had satisfied his predilection for teen-aged girls.

The new military rulers also put on display Eva's vast wardrobe of clothes and jewels. But strangely, in her case, the effect was only to gild her glittering reputation. Eva had never hidden her beautiful clothes and gems from her worshipping descamisados. It seemed not to matter to them that almost all of her wealth had been milked from the charities she had so ostentatiously championed.

Never give a sucker an even break!

Phineas is an unusual name. Biblically, it means 'he with a brazen mouth'. In the case of Phineas T. Barnum, the greatest showman the world has even seen, it was extremely apt.

Big-mouthed Barnum would tell the most outrageous lies to lure his American audiences. They were persuaded to pay to view his 'cherry-coloured cat' – only to find themselves staring incredulously at an ordinary black alley cat which, according to the sign, was 'the colour of *black* cherries'! They would queue to see 'the horse with its tail where its head should be'. Spectators would be led into a tent where a perfectly ordinary horse would be tethered in a stall – back to front, with its tail in the feeding trough!

Phineas Taylor Barnum, born July 5, 1810, lured millions of sensation seekers to his museums and circus tents by creating and exhibiting well-publicized fakes and phonies such as these.

There was his 'Feejee Mermaid' which he claimed had been fished from the Pacific in 1817. Thousands paid their 10 cents to see this marvellous freak that in reality was the result of a taxidermist's art and Barnum's imagination. The upper part of the mermaid was a monkey and the lower part a fish.

In 1841 Barnum opened the American Museum in New York. It housed a permanent exhibition of art, curiosities and natural history, and Barnum boasted: 'I mean people to talk about my museum, to exclaim over its wonders, to have men and women all over the country say that there is no place in the United States where so much can be seen for 25 cents as in Barnum's American Museum.'

Most of the exhibits really were remarkable . . . and quite genuine. There was a fantastic working model of the Niagara Falls and the first Punch and Judy show ever seen on that side of the Atlantic. There was also a live hippopotamus and a flea circus. But such was Barnum's distaste for plain speaking that he billed the hippo as 'the Great Behemoth of the Scriptures' and the fleas were advertised as 'insects that can draw carriages and carts'. Of course, the carriages and carts were suitably insect-sized.

Another of Barnum's attractions was an African elephant which had been a big draw in the London and Paris zoos. It was called Jumbo and it has given its name since to everything from jumboburgers to jumbo jets. It died in 1885 after being struck by a train during a tour of Canada.

At the other end of the size scale was mighty midget 'General' Tom Thumb.

Barnum's half-brother Philo mentioned to the showman that the five-year-old phenomenon was being exhibited at Bridgeport, Connecticut. Barnum dropped everything, raced to see the tiny fellow and signed him up on the spot to work for him at $3 a week.

Tom Thumb, born January 4, 1838, had weighed more than 9 pounds at birth and had developed normally until the age of six months. Since then he had not grown another inch. At the age of five he still stood just 2 ft 1 in tall.

Anyone else might have thought this extraordinary enough in itself. But not Barnum. He billed the lad as 'General Tom Thumb' a dwarf of 11 years of age, just arrived from England'. He trained the midget to be 'autocratic, impudent and regal' and made him learn by heart appalling, stilted, pun-filled speeches which he recited to enrapt audiences. Barnum dressed him at different times as Napoleon, a Roman gladiator and Cupid. Tom Thumb became Barnum's roving ambassador (and publicity agent) and during a British tour was even introduced to Queen Victoria.

Phineas T. Barnum is credited with coining the phrases 'There's a sucker born every minute' and 'Never give a sucker an even break'. It has also been suggested that the following famous words, generally attributed to Abraham Lincoln, were in fact spoken by Barnum: 'You can fool all the people some of the time and some of the people all of the time, but you cannot fool all the people all the time'.

Barnum learned these elementary rules of showmanship at an early age. In his home town of Bethel, Connecticut, he worked in a barter store, where goods were paid for not in cash but in kind. So much suspect merchandise was offered to the store that the rule of the house was to make sure of a good bargain by automatically offering faulty goods to the customer in return. 'Everything in that store,' said Barnum, 'was different from what it represented.' Burnt peas were sold as coffee beans and cotton offered in place of wool.

Barnum learnt a few useful lessons in Bethel. But he earned little money. So in 1843 he took his family to New York and established a sideshow. His very first exhibit secured his fortune. Posters plastered all over Manhattan announced:

'The greatest curiosity in the world, and the most interesting, particularly to Americans, is now exhibiting at the Saloon fronting on Broadway; Joice Heth, nurse to General George Washington, the father of our country, who has arrived at the astonishing age of 161 years, as authentic documents will prove, and in full possession of her mental faculties. She is cheerful and healthy though she weighs but 49 pounds. She relates many anecdotes of her young master . . .'

Barnum had not invented Joice Heth. She really existed. She was a hideously ugly old negress whom Barnum had come across in a sideshow in Philadelphia. She was blind and partly paralyzed, but Barnum borrowed money to buy her from her exhibitor and put her on show in New York. Joice would answer

Phineas Taylor Barnum, the great American showman

questions from the audience about her supposed career as Washington's nurse; any errors in her replies – and there were many – were excused on the grounds of her failing faculties.

So astute was her new owner that he even wrote anonymous letters to the newspapers calling into question the veracity of the old lady's claims. His reasoning, echoed by many a publicity man since, was that it is better to have people talking about you than not. Bad publicity is still publicity.

Joice Heth died in 1836. And Barnum, of course, found a way of making mileage of the event. He engaged a leading surgeon to perform an autopsy on the raddled old hag – in front of an invited audience. Unfortunately for Barnum, the surgeon's verdict was that Joice Heth was no more than 80 years old. Barnum was labelled a charlatan but he protested that he had been duped just like everyone else. It kept his name in the news!

Barnum's career in conmanship continued for a further half-century, with only one major setback. In 1865 fire destroyed his fabulous American Museum. A fireman single-handedly carried the 400-pound Fat Lady to safety but the 7 ft 11 in World's Tallest Woman had to be rescued by crane along with her friend the Human Skeleton. Wild animals escaped through the streets of New York and an orang-utan caused havoc in a nearby block of offices. It was big news, Barnum made sure of that.

The damage was put at $500,000 and Barnum was insured for only a tiny fraction of it. Yet by the time of his death in 1890, he had recouped his fortunes. He left $5 million – proving that 'there's a sucker born every minute'.

The bank robber aged nine

A nine-year-old freckle-faced youngster munched a chocolate bar in a New York court in March 1981, as a judge heard evidence that he was America's youngest bank robber.

The boy was said to have walked into a bank, pulled out a toy cap-pistol, held up a clerk, and walked out with just over $100.

If he hadn't been so small, the security cameras might have detected him in time. As it was, he skipped out a good few steps ahead of the guards. With the FBI and the police on his trail the boy spent all but $20 of his loot on hamburgers, chips, three picture shows and a wrist watch which played a tune. Then he turned himself in.

His lawyer said that the boy was brought up on a constant diet of TV crime shows. The day after watching *FBI* and *Policewoman* he got out his toy gun and went to the bank.

Cheats who bet on a racing 'certainty'

Doping horses and bribing jockeys was part and parcel of the American racing scene when gangsters fancied a flutter. Bookmakers refused to accept bets from the most notorious race-fixers, but in 1921 they fell for a coup orchestrated by one of Chicago's crime kings – and it was all above board.

Arnold Rothstein was at New York's Belmont Track when he had the brainwave that was to land him one of the biggest legitimate killings in racing history. Surveying the crowds clustered round the bookies, he realized the men taking the bets would be too busy to think clearly as the big race action hotted up. He turned to trainer Max Hirsch, and said: 'What have we got running?'

The only horse with a real possibility of winning was a five-year-old called Sidereal, but Hirsch, planning to scratch him for a bigger race the following week, had left him behind in the stables.

'Get him here,' snapped Rothstein. 'I'll get the money organized.'

The gangster took no chances that his men would be recognized. He borrowed 40 runners from acquaintances who owed him favours. They spread the bets through all the on-course bookmakers in small amounts.

Slowly the horse's odds dropped from 25–1 to 15–1. Then, five minutes before the off, a second wave of bets was laid. The odds crashed to 3–1, then 8–5, as bookmakers at last realized they had been caught.

There was nobody with whom they could lay off their bets, since all faced a heavy payout – nobody, that is, except Rothstein.

He agreed to accept bets worth $125,000 at 8–5, which guaranteed him against loss. If Sidereal won, he collected $850,000. In the unlikely event of it losing, he still made $40,000.

Sidereal romped home in the six-furlong sprint. Rothstein celebrated by going on to a poker game – and winning another $50,000.

The 1844 Derby at Epsom was the scene of an audacious coup on the other side of the Atlantic. Twenty-nine horses went into the frame that year for the premier classic of the English flat-racing season. Favourites were The Ugly Buck, recent winner of the 2,000 Guineas, and Colonel Jonathan Peel's entries, Orlando and Ionian.

A fancied dark horse, however, was Mr A. Wood's Running Rein. It had won an important race for two-year-olds at Newmarket eight months earlier, when owned by Mr A. L. Goodman. And though there had been an objection then from Lord Rutland, who claimed the horse was at least a year older than stated, it was overruled through lack of evidence.

A few days before the Epsom race, stewards received a letter from a group of racegoers led by Lord George Bentinck, second son of the Duke of Portland. It said there were strong doubts about whether Mr Wood's colt was really Running Rein, and urged the stewards to demand proof of identity and age. By a curious coincidence, a similar complaint was lodged by Lord Maidstone against another horse in the field, Leander.

The stewards insisted that, as far as they were concerned, everything was in order. But the two owners were warned to expect an objection if their horses were first past the post. Neither withdrew their mounts, and both lined up at the start on the big day. A sudden rush of bets on Running Rein had cut the colt's odds to 10–1.

Leander made the early running, but after a half of a mile he was overtaken – and kicked – by Running Rein, who held on to beat Orlando by three-quarters of a length.

Orlando's owner, Colonel Peel, immediately slapped in his objection, claiming, on evidence supplied by Lord George Bentinck, that Running Rein was really a horse called Maccabaeus, and that, contrary to the limit on entries to three-year-olds, the horse was four years of age.

Jockey Club stewards upheld the protest, and awarded the race and stakes to Orlando. But Mr Wood refused to let the matter rest there. He decided to contest the decision by taking Colonel Peel to court at Westminster. On July 1, before Baron Alderson and a special jury, he claimed the horse's pedigree was a true one. He lost his plea because he could no longer produce the horse. The court was told it had vanished.

The true villain of the piece was not Mr Wood but former owner Abraham Levi Goodman.

Lord George Bentinck's detective work had revealed that Goodman had been owner of both Running Rein and Maccabaeus, and had sold the latter to Wood as Running Rein – on condition he ran him in the Derby. Since Maccabaeus was a far superior runner, and looked almost identical, he hoped to cash in at long odds. In the event Goodman had backed the horse to win £100,000 and then fled abroad when the row blew up.

Crime fits penalty

A burly centre-forward, sent off for violent conduct during a soccer match, said, 'If I'm to be sent off for that I may as well commit it.' He then hit the referee in the face. A London court fined him £20.

But incredibly, a second fraud attempt had been carried out in the race. Leander, who had to be destroyed after Running Rein's kick, was also a 'ringer'.

Ironically, if Leander had finished second, the Running Rein coup might have succeeded. Leander's owners would hardly have objected – since, at five, their horse was *two* years above the race's age limit!

Greyhound racing has also had its share of scandals as crooks and con-men have attempted to bash the bookies. Most have failed. But at London's White City on December 8, 1945, a gang pulled off the most spectacular swindle in the history of the sport. They got clean away with more than £100,000.

It was the 9.30 race, the last on the card, and second favourite Fly Bessie led at the first bend, closely followed by Jimmy's Chicken. Then, to the amazement of the 16,000 crowd, the dog began to swerve drunkenly and lose ground. One by one, the others also started stumbling . . . all except the rank outsider, a white hound called Bald Truth.

He streaked home 15 lengths ahead of the second dog, with favourite Victory Speech trailing in fourth.

No one was more amazed than Bald Truth's owner, Colonel B.C. 'Jock' Hartley, wartime director of the Army Sports Board. The dog had only been brought in as a late substitute to increase the field to five, and his £2 bet on it was ruled more by his heart than his head.

He sat speechless as fans shouted and growled, and track officials delayed making the official announcements. Surely it would be declared 'no race'.

But there was nothing the officials could do. No. 4 went up in lights; Bald Truth was the winner. Bets would be paid.

The affair, however, was far from over. Chief Inspector Robert Fabian of Scotland Yard was called in to investigate the coup, which followed a series of minor frauds at tracks around the country.

Slowly the pieces of the puzzle were fitted into place. The swindlers had used a dope called cholocretone. It was untraceable in pre-race examinations, but had an alcoholic effect as the dogs heated up during a race.

Investigators decided that the culprit had crept into a disused kennel, used to store straw and timber. Then, when all eyes were on the track during the penultimate race, he had crawled out, fed drugged pieces of fish to all the dogs except Bald Truth – the only white dog in the field – and returned to his kennel until the coast was clear.

Meanwhile the rest of the gang were placing bets with bookies all over the country and on the course, bringing the price down from 33–1 to 11–2 by the start.

Despite a £1,000 reward offered by the Greyhound Racing Association, the swindlers were never caught.

EPSOM.
DERBY DAY
18 44

Derby Day at Epsom in 1844

Years later a crooked businessman, politician and philanthropist, Horatio Bottomley, attempted the most ingenious racing coup of all time. But, sadly for him, it was no more than an attempt.

Bottomley, a wheeler-dealer trader born in London's tough East End, bought his way into parliament through much-publicized charity work. He financed Australian gold-mines and made £3 million by juggling funds between his many companies, despite being served with 67 writs of bankruptcy.

He was also a racehorse owner and an inveterate gambler. And he knew that the only way to be certain of winning a race was to own every horse running.

That, Bottomley decided, was exactly what he would do!

The schemer scoured Europe for a country where racing rules were lax and where there was a racecourse to suit his devious purposes. He eventually chose Blankenberg, a Belgian seaside resort, where the course meandered through sand dunes, often obscuring the field from the spectators.

There were to be six horses in the race, and all were owned by Bottomley. The politician hired dozens of associates to place bets on his behalf – bets on the precise order in which the six horses would romp home.

The six jockeys were, of course, also in the pay of Bottomley who instructed them to sort themselves out into the required order as they raced off.

On the day of the race, disaster befell. A thick mist blew in from the sea and the jockeys could not even see one another. Their leader's startled cries to his fellow jockeys were muffled by the mist – and the six of them galloped to the finishing line in entirely the wrong order.

The betting 'coup' of the century ended as a fiasco. Bottomley lost a fortune, the first in a line of major setbacks that ended with a seven-year jail sentence for fraud in 1921.

Tout hits censor trouble

John Trevelyan, a man with a special interest in films, was accosted by a tout as he left his office in London's Soho.

Tout: 'How much would you like to see a blue movie?'

Trevelyan: How much will you pay me to see it?'

Tout: 'But you don't understand. You have to pay me to see it'.

Trevelyan: 'No, you don't understand. You have to pay me. It's my job.'

Tout: What do you do, then?'

Trevelyan: 'I'm head of the British Board of Film Censors.'

The unbelievable Horatio Bottomley

As we have seen from the unsuccessful racecourse fraud described in the previous chapter, Horatio Bottomley had the gift of the gab. He could charm people into parting with their money – and often talk his way out of trouble afterwards.

Bottomley was born in London's East End in 1860 but he rose to become a Member of Parliament and a conman with few rivals.

From an early age he knew what he wanted – money, fame, women and a successful political career. After first working as a solicitor's clerk and then a shorthand writer at the Law Courts in London, he turned his attentions to making money – big money – by fraud.

Together with friends, he launched a publishing company. Through another friend he bought some properties, including a printing works in Devon, for more than £200,000. Then he sold them to the publishing company for £325,000.

The trouble was that most of the properties were worthless. Bottomley knew it but the directors of the publishing company had been taken in by him.

Charged with fraud and sent for trial, Bottomley defended himself with such skill that he won. He so impressed the trial judge that he suggested that Bottomley should consider becoming a lawyer!

Bottomley's next move was into the Australian gold boom. By 1897 he had made a small fortune from promoting gold mines. Despite his success, his firms failed regularly and he was constantly being served with writs for bankruptcy.

Yet the public continued to pour their money into his ventures.

His method was simple. He would start a company, declare high dividends and as a result the price of the shares would rocket. Then he and his conspirators would sell the shares at the inflated price.

When the company started to sink, as it invariably did, up would pop Bottomley with a new company, offering to take over the old firm, backed, of course, by more funds from the unsuspecting shareholders.

Bottomley was instrumental in founding the *Financial Times* newspaper and the jingoistic magazine *John Bull*; he was elected to Parliament to represent the London constituency of Hackney South.

Although married, he kept a succession of young mistresses in love nests throughout the country.

At his home in Upper Dicker, near Eastbourne, Sussex, he lived the life of the local squire. But in 1912 he suffered a major setback when forced to resign from

Horatio Bottomley in 1927

Parliament because of a bankruptcy case.

Undeterred, he carried on as usual with his business enterprises and when hostilities broke out in 1914 used his demagogic powers in *John Bull* to support the war effort. He also made stirring recruiting speeches up and down the country – for which he charged a fee!

In 1918, with the war over, he was re-elected to Parliament for his old constituency. One year later he launched his biggest swindle and sealed his own fate . . .

Victory Bonds had been issued by the Government with a face value of £5, although investors could buy them at a discount price of £4 15 shillings. For ordinary working people this was still a lot of money; so Bottomley launched his Victory Bond Club. People were able to invest as little or as much as they wanted and the club would buy the bonds for them.

Bottomley was hailed as the friend of the little man – an image he loved to cultivate. What the investors didn't know was that their hero had siphoned off about £150,000 of the estimated half-million pounds that had flowed into the club in six short months.

The beginning of the end came when Bottomley started and then dropped a criminal libel case against one of his former partners, Reuben Bigland, who had accused him of a swindle.

By this time, the Chancery Court was investigating his empire and in 1922 he was prosecuted at the Old Bailey for fraudulent conversion of the funds of the Victory Bond Club.

This time Bottomley's glib tongue didn't sway the jury. After hearing evidence that he had used the money from the club to pay off £10,000 worth of debts, spent £15,000 on his burning passion for horse-racing and another £15,000 to buy and exhibit a German submarine, they took just 30 minutes to find him guilty. He was sentenced to seven years penal servitude but was released on licence in 1926. He tried to restore his old lifestyle, but in vain.

Horatio Bottomley, ex-millionaire, died in poverty in 1933.

Tea break

A woman who was picking blackberries from a cluster of brambles growing along the wall of London's Wormwood Scrubs prison noticed a rope and a wooden ladder drop down the side of the wall. Three men followed. 'I didn't raise the alarm,' said the woman. 'They told me they were nipping out for a cup of tea and planned to go back later.'

Going cheap – some of the world's best-loved landmarks

In 1925, within the space of a few weeks, a plausible Scottish rogue named Arthur Furguson sold off three of London's best-known landmarks to gullible American tourists. Buckingham Palace went for £2,000, Big Ben fetched £1,000 and Nelson's Column was sold for £6,000.

That anyone could fall for such obvious confidence tricks seems beyond belief. Yet Furguson was a past master at the art of gentle persuasion, thanks to his training as an actor. He appeared in repertory company melodramas throughout Scotland and northern England, once acting the role of an American conned by a trickster. Perhaps it was this part which inspired him to move south to London to try his hand in earnest at the con game.

The ex-actor would take up his position near a London monument, studying it with an air of rapt concentration. Soon a tourist would make an inquiry about the history of the monument and Furguson would engage him in conversation.

Once, while pacing around Trafalgar Square, he was approached by an American tourist from Iowa. Yes, said Furguson, the tower in the centre of the square was Nelson's Column, erected in honour of the great admiral. But sadly, he said, it would not be there for long. It was to be sold and dismantled along with several other landmarks to help repay Britain's vast war loan from the United States. And it was he, Furguson, who as a ministry official had been given the task of arranging the sale.

Yes indeed, Furguson informed the gentleman from Iowa, he was reluctantly authorized to accept a bid for the column even at this late stage. Furthermore, since the tourist was so obviously a lover of great art, he could arrange for him to jump the queue.

A cheque for £6,000 promptly changed hands and the American was left with a receipt and the address of a demolition company. It was only when the demolition company refused to consider carrying out the job of knocking down one of London's most historic sights that the American at last began to suspect that he had been taken for a ride.

Furguson used much the same ploy to dispose of the Big Ben clock tower and the King's royal residence of Buckingham Palace. Then, encouraged by his success in extracting cash from trusting Americans, he emigrated late in 1925 to enjoy this fount of easy money.

Within a few weeks he was back in action. In Washington DC, he met a Texas cattleman admiring the White House. Pretending to be a government agent, Furguson spun a slender yarn about how the administration was looking for ways of cutting costs. Now, if the Texan would care to lease the White House at a knockdown rent of $100,000 a year . . .? Furguson was in business again.

Moving on to New York, the wily Scotsman explained to an Australian visitor that, because of a proposed scheme for widening New York Harbour, the Statue of Liberty would have to be dismantled and sold. A great loss to the US, but would it not look grand in Sydney Harbour . . .? The Australian immediately began to raise the $100,000 that the con-man asked for the statue. But his bankers advised him to make a few further inquiries, and the police were tipped off.

This time Furguson had really slipped up. He had allowed the Australian visitor to take a souvenir snapshot of himself with the Statue of Liberty in the background. Police were immediately able to identify him as a man they had been watching.

Furguson was arrested, and a court sentenced him to five years in jail. When he came out, the master-hoaxer retired from the ancient monuments business and, until his death in 1938, lived in California – languishing in luxury on his ill-gotten gains.

The Balfour snowball

Jabez Balfour started with nothing and ended with nothing. But in between he made millions – by getting the public to invest cash in fraudulent companies.

Balfour became one of the most respected men of the late Victorian era. He was a Justice of the Peace, Mayor of the London suburb of Croydon and Member of Parliament for Burnley, Lancashire. He was on the point of landing a top Government job when his empire crashed and he was forced to flee the country.

Balfour is said to have originated the snowballing technique (whereby one company finances another) when, in 1868, he set up the Liberator Building Society. Over the next few years there followed a succession of companies such as the Lands Allotment Company, George Newman and Co. and the Real

Jabez Spencer Balfour

Estates Co. In 1882 he founded the London and General Bank with the main aim of processing the mass of dubious cheques that flowed from one into another of his companies.

While his companies bought and sold land and properties to one another – always of course with huge profits for Balfour and his cronies – the subscriptions poured in from the unsuspecting public.

The small investors believed in Balfour. Every year, regular as clockwork, they got eight per cent interest on their savings. Each time Balfour floated a new company it would be oversubscribed as the public flocked to invest.

Balfour was a success and they wanted to be part of it. What they didn't know was that their dividends were being paid out of new subscriptions and were not derived from any real company profits.

As the years passed, the snowball gathered speed and Balfour's business transactions became more and more complicated, his money-spinning schemes even bolder. He not only captivated his devoted investors but also dominated his business colleagues and employees, some of whom were genuinely honest men, others out-and-out villains.

Unlike some of his fellow con-men, there had never been a breath of scandal about Balfour. He had had a strict non-conformist upbringing and he carried this image of trust and respectability into his business and political life.

Large snowballs may take time to melt – but melt they do.

Suddenly in 1892, one of his companies collapsed, owing £8 million. It came out of the blue, quite stunning the financial world, so accustomed to Balfour's successes. Investors, and indeed the entire nation, were shocked at the news.

The only person not caught by surprise was Jabez Balfour. He was well prepared. While Britain was counting the cost of his 20 years of scheming and stealing, he was heading for South America, where he disappeared for three years.

Then, unhappily for him, he was recognized by a visitor to the little Chilean town of Salta. The man reported his discovery to the British Consul who eventually, after a long struggle, managed to extradite Balfour back to Britain to stand trial at the Old Bailey.

Some of the top legal brains of the time were lined up against Balfour. Masses of papers and legal documents were piled high on the court benches as they fought to show how he had swindled his way to millions.

It didn't take long for the jury to decide that he was guilty. He was sent to prison for 14 years with the words of the judge, Mr Justice Bruce, ringing in his ears: 'You will never be able to shut out the cry of the widows and orphans you have ruined.'

Balfour served his time and was planning to start up in business again when he died of a heart attack.

Bank busters extraordinary

Innumerable con-men have tried and failed to get the better of the mighty Bank of England. But it took four American financial wizards just six weeks to swindle 'The Old Lady of Threadneedle Street' out of £100,000 at the height of the Victorian era.

Their method was simple and it made George Macdonnel, Edwin Noyes, George Bidwell and his brother, Austin, rich men. But not for long.

They took advantage of a banking procedure that differed from the American system. The Bank of England had a well-established business in buying bills of exchange at discount rates.

The owner of a bill could take it to the Bank and exchange it for cash before it was officially due to be bought back by the finance house that issued it to raise capital. The Bank kept the bills until the end of the financial quarter when they were due to be repaid in full by the finance houses.

Macdonnel discovered that the Bank did not check whether bills were genuine before buying, as was done at home in America. He knew that a forgery would not be discovered until the end of a financial quarter, allowing the conspirators plenty of time to get away.

He sent word to his friends, the Bidwells, who joined him in London to launch the scheme in November 1872. Austin Bidwell opened an account under a false name at the Bank of England's branch in London's smart West End. Austin Bidwell must have been a very persuasive character, or the branch officials very gullible, for the Bank did not even check his identity, references or address. They seemed more than happy to have £2,000 on deposit from the smooth-talking American 'businessman'.

The conspirators' next move was to pay £8,000 in foreign currency into Bidwell's account. Any doubts entertained by the branch manager, Colonel Peregrine Francis, were surely allayed by the knowledge that his American customer was credit-worthy. Bidwell announced that he was planning to open a

---

What a gas!
Ronald Carr's gas-meter fiddle was a double disaster. He altered the meter the wrong way, so he ended up paying more instead of less. And in court at Rochdale, Lancashire, he was fined £75 for trying to steal the gas.

factory in Birmingham and might need to be granted credit. Francis quickly agreed. In order to strengthen confidence in Bidwell, the conspirators set about trading with genuine bills of exchange.

By the New Year of 1873 the time was right for the conspirators to move in for the kill. Bidwell informed Francis that his Birmingham factory had started to thrive and that he expected to be involved in some large financial transactions over the next few weeks.

Meanwhile, the men had been making faithful copies of their genuine bills of exchange. At this point they brought in from America Edwin Noyes, the fourth conspirator. His task was to present the bills of exchange and to help the gang change gold sovereigns for paper money which could be transported more easily.

In the six weeks up to the end of February 1873, Noyes exchanged a total of 94 bills, totalling £102,000. The plot came to light when the gang thought they still had three weeks of safety before the end of the financial quarter. In his haste to forge exchange bills, Macdonnel had failed to put dates on two of them. Bank manager Francis returned the bills to the finance houses that had supposedly issued them, to find that he had been duped. Noyes was the only member of the gang still in Britain and he was arrested as he went to close his bank account. Austin Bidwell was arrested in Cuba, his brother George was caught in Edinburgh and Macdonnel was extradited from New York.

When the case came to trial at the Old Bailey in August 1873, the evidence against the four men was so overwhelming that the defence lawyers did not even bother to address the jury. All four men were sentenced to penal servitude for life. Austin Bidwell was released after 17 years, Macdonnel and Noyes after 18 years. But George Bidwell, a con-man to the last, convinced the prison doctor that he was near to death and was released on compassionate grounds after only six years in jail. As soon as he was released, he made a remarkable recovery from his mystery illness.

A bevy of bottoms

Dozens of seemingly unrelated people received special invitations to a surprise dinner at a top London hotel. Nobody knew anyone else at the dinner but, as they introduced each other, they discovered that the guest list was made up of Winterbottoms, Sidebottoms, Littlebottoms, Witherbottoms, Highbottoms, Lowbottoms and plain ordinary Bottoms. One of these many Bottoms had called all the other Bottoms together for a joke.

The bouncing Czech who sold the Eiffel Tower at a knock-down price!

The idea came to Victor Lustig in a flash. There he was lounging in his Paris hotel room in March 1925 idly perusing the newspapers when he came across an item that made his eyes widen. The Eiffel Tower, said the report, was in need of major renovation. It had even been suggested that the city's most famous landmark should be demolished and rebuilt. . . .

To an artist, inspiration can come in a flash – and Victor Lustig was nothing if not an artist. The only difference was that his art was outside the law – he was a genius at deception. And the news item in that Paris paper opened up the opportunity for the coolest confidence trick of the present century.

First, Lustig (or 'Count Lustig', as he styled himself) acquired some printed notepaper from the French Ministry of Posts, which was responsible for maintaining the monument, and invited five French businessmen to a secret meeting at the Crillon Hotel, Paris.

When they arrived, they were ushered into a private suite by Lustig's 'ministerial secretary', a fellow con-man named Robert Tourbillon. The five were then sworn to secrecy and told the terrible news: that the Eiffel Tower was in a dangerous condition and would have to be pulled down.

There was sure to be a public outcry over the demolition of such a well-loved national monument, so the French government had to ensure total security. This was why five highly respectable and trusted members of the business community had been specially chosen for their loyalty and discretion.

The five flattered fools fell for Lustig's ruse completely. They each agreed to submit tenders for the value of the 7,000 tons of scrap metal that would be produced by demolishing the tower. Then they went away to make their calculations.

Lustig, however, had already picked out his candidate, a scrap metal merchant named André Poisson, one of the provincial nouveaux riches anxious to make a name for himself in the Paris business world. When, within the week, all five bids were in, Lustig accepted Poisson's and invited him back to the hotel to give him the good news.

It was then that the con-man played his master-stroke. He asked Poisson for a bribe to help the deal go smoothly through official channels. The duped dealer agreed willingly, and gave the back-hander in cash. If he had ever had any suspicions, they were now allayed. After all, a demand for a bribe meant that Count Victor must be from the Ministry!

Poisson handed over a banker's draft. In return, he received an utterly worthless bill of sale.

Lustig and Tourbillon were out of the country within 24 hours. But they stayed abroad only long enough to realize that the outcry they had expected to follow their fraud had not materialized. Poisson was so ashamed at being taken for a ride that he never reported the hoax to the police.

The 'count' and his partner returned to Paris and repeated the trick. They sold the Eiffel Tower all over again to another gullible scrap merchant. This time the man did go to the police, and the con-men fled. They were never brought to justice, and they never revealed just how much money they had got away with.

To a man like Lustig, proud of his art, selling the Eiffel Tower not once but twice was the pinnacle of a long career in confidence trickery. Born in Czechoslovakia in 1890, he had worked his way through Europe, using 22 aliases and being arrested 45 times.

He emigrated to America – but found the pickings so rich among the wealthy passengers on his Atlantic liner that he returned to make the transatlantic trip over and over again!

During the roaring Twenties, when 'making a fast buck' seemed to be all that life was about, Lustig preyed on the avarice of the greedy and gullible.

His cardinal rule when setting up a 'prospect' was to listen. Lustig never sold hard; he always let his victim do the talking, while the con-man showed deep interest. He would seek out his victim's political views and religious preferences and concur wholeheartedly to make him feel he had found a kindred spirit. But at the end of the day, the most crucial common interest would always be money.

Rags-to-riches multi-millionaire Herbert Loller had amassed all the money he could ever need. But he still wanted more, however dubiously it was acquired. Lustig demonstrated to him a machine which duplicated banknotes, and sold it to him for $25,000. Of course, it never worked. But by the time Loller discovered the fact, Lustig had disappeared to the next town, with another name and a new identity.

In the bootlegging days, Lustig insinuated himself into the company of Al Capone. It took a very brave, or perhaps foolhardy, man to tangle with the Chicago gangster, but Lustig actually tried to swindle him out of $50,000. The con-man told him he had a system that would ensure he doubled his money on Wall Street within two months.

Lustig took the money but after a while even he got cold feet and returned the $50,000 intact to Capone. The gangster must have taken a liking to the genial

Victor Lustig

fraud, because he forgave him and even gave him a $5,000 'tip' for his troubles.

Lustig's associations with the Capone gang continued for several years and led the trickster into an area of crime in which he found himself out of his class. That crime was counterfeiting.

By 1934 a special team of federal agents had been assigned to capture Lustig and his old Capone associate William Watts and to stem the flow of forged $100 bills which the pair were producing at the rate of $100,000 a month.

After tapping their phones for several months, the agents thought they had enough evidence. The pair were arrested and, although Lustig offered to reveal the whereabouts of all the counterfeit engraving plates if he were freed, he was thrown into New York's dreaded Tombs prison.

He didn't remain there long. One morning wardens found his cell empty and a sheet missing. They discovered it dangling from a window. Lustig had gone to ground again.

The master fraud may well have learned his lesson by now. After his jailbreak he fled to Pittsburgh and took on identity number 23 – that of quiet, retiring Mr Robert Miller. But luck was against him. A tip-off led police to his apartment and, after arrest number 47, he was put back in jail to await trial.

The outcome was the worst Lustig could have expected. In December 1945 he was found guilty of distributing a staggering $134,000,000 in counterfeit bills and was sentenced to 20 years imprisonment – the first part of it to be served on the escape-proof island of Alcatraz.

'Count' Victor Lustig, king of the con-men, served only 11 years of his sentence. He died in Springfield Prison, Missouri, in March 1947.

But what of Lustig's partner, Robert Arthur Tourbillon, the man who acted out the role of his 'secretary' in the greatest confidence trick of the century, the sale of the Eiffel Tower? Tourbillon, or 'Dapper Dan Colins' as the police knew him, had almost as amazing a career as Lustig himself.

Born in 1885, Tourbillon's first job was as a lion-tamer in a French circus. His act was called the Circle of Death and it involved his riding a bicycle around a pride of lions. Circus life was too tame for him, however, and at an early age he turned to crime.

He was 23 when he emigrated to America and was 31 when he first went to jail – for, of all things, 'white slavery'. He emerged from prison four years later determined to stick to the one crime he was best at: fraud. Until then, he had been known among the criminal fraternity as The Rat (after his initials) but he now styled himself 'Dapper Dan Collins', bought himself the smartest clothes in New York and set sail for his homeland, France.

He lived for several years in Paris, mainly off the proceeds of rich, old ladies who fell for the Casanova charm of this suave 'American'. In 1925 he and Victor Lustig pulled off their Eiffel Tower fraud and afterwards both men went to ground.

Further bad luck brought Tourbillon to the end of the road. Two American detectives who were in Paris with an extradition warrant for another crook heard about the suspicious exploits of 'Dapper Dan', sought him out – and recognized 'the Rat'. They arrested him and returned him to New York aboard the liner *France*. It was an amazing voyage. Tourbillon was given the freedom of the ship and, on his money, the trip turned into one large party for passengers, crew, criminal and detectives.

Amazingly, when the liner reached New York and Tourbillon was arraigned before a court, the robbery charges that had been brought against him failed to stick and he was freed. But not for long. . . .

In 1929, Tourbillon was charged with defrauding a New Jersey farmer out of $30,000 savings and was jailed for two years. He served 16 months and left jail vowing to return to France. Whether he did so or not, no one knows – for after speaking to reporters outside the jail, Tourbillon was never heard of again.

The match king who struck it rich

Ivar Kreugar struck it rich and created one of the biggest financial empires ever seen. The wily Swede, who captured almost three-quarters of the world's supply of safety matches, built his empire on a gigantic fraud.

He conned millions of pounds from investors and banks in Europe and America before the bubble burst in 1932 and Kreugar – the man the world knew as The Match King – shot himself through the heart in his Paris apartment.

Kreugar was already a rich man when he embarked on his mammoth fraud. Born in Kalmar, Sweden, in 1880, he went to America when he was 19. When he returned to Sweden in 1908, he had amassed a tidy sum from dealing in South African gold and diamond shares.

Once home, he went into partnership with a friend called Toll. Between them they set up a building company which went from strength to strength, using many new techniques Kreugar had picked up while in America.

By 1914 Kreugar and Toll were wealthy. Then, suddenly, Kreugar quit and took over his family's ailing match business. He had taken the first steps on the rocky road to fame, fortune and suicide.

Kreugar was ruthless. By 1917 he had created the Swedish Match Company, of which he was president, by taking over or crushing all his competitors.

From this position of strength, he began to build a succession of companies. Each one was tied to the next by such a complicated web that only Kreugar knew how it all strung together. He wrote his own company reports and declared the profits and dividends.

Such was the success of his companies that investors fought to put their money in. What they didn't know was that most of the high dividends they received on their investments came not from profits but from money people had already invested in other Kreugar companies.

Kreugar had such tight control of his empire that everyone believed his valuation of its profits. It was almost impossible for anyone to unravel the deliberately complex figures in his reports.

Kreugar wanted desperately to be known as the world's Number One wheeler-dealer. He was already leading a frantic life of fast cars and mistresses in many European capitals when he decided to build himself a massive headquarters in Stockholm.

It was a huge commercial palace full of marble columns and fountains. His own office was magnificent with rich carpets, mahogany panels, beautiful decorations and a bank of telephones on his desk to impress even the most important of clients.

By 1921 Kreugar had established such a reputation and had such vast reserves of money available to him through investors and bank loans that he could embark on his final plan – to control the world's match market.

He knew what he wanted and he didn't care how he got it. If a rival company wouldn't sell, Kreugar either cut off their supplies of raw materials or sent in the thugs on his payroll to persuade or blackmail them into submission.

By 1922 the match industries of Sweden, Norway, Denmark, Finland and Belgium were in his hands.

In countries where the match industries were state-owned he simply offered to make loans to the governments in return for the right to total control of the industry. To do this he needed money – many millions, all of which he raised in America by persuading bankers and private investors to sink their cash into yet another of his new companies.

Much of the money went straight into Swiss banks. Not because he wanted to steal it. He just wanted it under his control so that he could use it as and when he wanted.

Over the next two years he loaned more than £150 million to 20 countries, giving him control of 65 per cent of the world's match production.

But the Wall Street stock market crash of 1929 sealed the fate of the Match King. As credit began to dry up all over the world, so many of Kreugar's clients who had borrowed money began to miss their repayments.

At the same time Kreugar still had to find the money for the governments to whom he had promised loans. He had to retain the confidence of his investors and creditors or his financial edifice would collapse.

He even resorted to straight trickery to get new loans from banks, using a receipt from one bank to get credit from another.

The final reckoning came in 1931 when he tried to sell one of his companies to the giant American-owned ITT corporation. Their investigation of the company books showed £7 million was missing. They called off the deal.

When the news broke, everyone wanted their money out of the Kreugar companies.

The Match King tried desperately to keep up the price of his shares by buying them with millions of pounds of his own money. But it was to no avail. The following year, when he heard the Swedish Bank were investigating one of his phoney deals involving forged Italian bonds, he went to his Paris flat and shot himself.

It has been said that Kreugar never intended to keep the money he conned for his personal use. If that had been the case, he would simply have disappeared when things started to go wrong instead of spending his personal fortune trying to prop up his empire.

No, say many who knew him, he just wanted to be Number One.

Titles for sale

Maundy Gregory made a mint out of selling titles to people desperate for honours. But the man who rubbed shoulders with kings, prime ministers and earls ended his years in exile and died in a wartime German hospital.

The artful conman was born in 1877, the elder of two sons of a Hampshire clergyman. His first job was as a teacher but he gave that up and went on the stage as an actor. He had some moderate success for several years before deciding to go into the business side of the theatre.

So in 1907 he opened up an office in London's Charing Cross Road as an impresario. His career in theatre management was short-lived. After two years he backed a musical extravaganza which collapsed, leaving him broke.

But although his business was in ruins, Gregory had made many useful contacts in high places. The scene was set for the Honours salesman supreme to move into the big time.

Like most conmen, Gregory oozed charm and confidence. He was kind and considerate to anyone he thought could help him, sometimes showering them with gifts. He dressed the part, too, with a diamond watch chain strung across his well-tailored suits.

He built up his image as a man of influence by launching a magazine, *The Whitehall Gazette and St James Review* – which was stoutly anti-Communist – and starting his own club, The Ambassador, in Conduit Street, London. Then he set up a palatial office in Parliament Street, close to Downing Street, with a commissionaire at the front door dressed deliberately as a Government messenger.

No one knew exactly where he fitted into the Establishment, but his victims were too flushed with the possibility of a knighthood or a peerage to enquire too deeply.

His con-trick was made that much easier by the fact that shortly after the end of the First World War the Prime Minister, Lloyd George, was openly selling off honours in a bid to boost his political funds – and to make sure he had plenty of supporters in the House of Lords.

Gregory had two ways of relieving his victims of their cash.

His first was to discover through his many contacts who was already in line for a knighthood or a baronetcy. Then he would check discreetly to see who on the list wanted an honour enough to pay for it. His rates varied but he usually charged £10,000 for a knighthood, £35,000 for a baronetcy and about £50,000 for a peerage.

The victim would be sent a letter suggesting a meeting to discuss a matter of great confidence. Many paid up, completely unaware that they would have got the honour anyway.

Plaster cast

Police in Sydney, Australia, ordered a drink-driving clampdown in 1970. They were keeping a discreet watch on one downtown club when they saw a customer stagger out of the door and fall down the front steps.

He picked himself up, stumbled to the car park, spent a few minutes trying to unlock the car, got in, crashed the gears and took off.

A police car followed, stopped him and gave him a roadside breath test. The test was negative. They took him to the police station for another test. Also negative.

Meanwhile the car park outside the club emptied as members drove off in a hurry. Puzzled police escorted the 'drunk' back to the car, and asked what he did for a living.

'I'm a professional decoy,' he said.

Just one call

A robber in Reno, Nevada, agreed to let a garage owner he was holding up make just one phone call. The owner called the police, who arrested the young raider on the forecourt.

His second method was to look for a rich businessman who he knew would pay for an honour and then use his contacts in the Government to get the man's name on the Honours List.

Gregory had a field day until a change of Government spelled disaster. The Conservatives, under Stanley Baldwin, were determined to stamp out the trading in honours and passed a new Act of Parliament in 1925 which made it illegal.

Undeterred, Gregory carried on as usual, but the big guns of the Conservative Party were out to stop him. They even infiltrated one of their top officials into his organization to get a list of people to whom Gregory had promised honours.

Then, in 1933, Gregory made a big mistake. He offered Commander Edward Leake a knighthood for £10,000. Gregory was arrested and tried at Bow Street Court under the 1925 Act. The Commander told the court how he had received a letter from a complete stranger offering an introduction to Gregory, who over one of his usual expensive lunches made his proposal.

Gregory told him how it would cost money to open the right doors to get him a knighthood and how he had done it many times in the past. The Commander went straight to Scotland Yard.

Gregory at first pleaded not guilty but later changed his plea to guilty. He was sentenced to two months in jail.

No further evidence was offered – and many people in high places breathed easily again. A long-drawn-out trial could have meant the exposure of many prominent people who had already done business with Gregory.

After his release, Gregory survived another scandal, over the mysterious death of Edith Rosse, a woman he had been living with for some years, before he slipped out of the country to live in Paris. There he remained as Sir Arthur Gregory until he died aged 64 in a German hospital in 1941.

Chapter Three

Artful Tricksters

'The fear of the criminal is the same as the fear of
the artist: both are terrified of exposure.
It is basic to their nature.'
Richard Linder

The great Howard Hughes rip-off

It was billed as the publishing coup of the decade. But it proved to be the literary hoax of the century. The project was the 'autobiography' of the richest eccentric in the world, the legendary multi-millionaire recluse Howard Hughes.

The man behind this ambitious venture was an author named Clifford Irving, a man who, despite never having met Hughes, planned to write the mystery man's life story and sell the book to a publisher as being Hughes's own words.

Hughes was a sick, semi-senile man, possibly drug-addicted, and a fanatical recluse. He would allow nobody near him apart from the tight circle of Mormon male nurses who tended his needs in a succession of hotel-suites around the world.

Clifford Irving was an altogether different character. Born in New York in 1930, he was an incurable adventurer. Educated at art college and Cornell University, he sailed the Atlantic and lived with California's beatniks and Kashmir's drop-outs. He ended his ramblings when he married a pretty, slim blonde named Edith and settled down to write on the Mediterranean island of Ibiza.

His New York publishers, McGraw-Hill, encouraged him in his work and he attained moderate success. It was to McGraw-Hill that Irving turned when he wanted to sell his 'publishing coup of the century'.

Irving's amazing lie was this. . . . He had sent a copy of one of his own books to Howard Hughes for his critical comments. Hughes had replied in the kindest terms. The two had hit it off so well that Irving had boldly suggested 'ghosting' a Howard Hughes autobiography. And, to Irving's surprise, the old recluse had agreed.

McGraw-Hill fell for the bait. They agreed that Hughes would receive a hefty payment for allowing a series of tape-recorded interviews with Irving. And, of course, the author himself was to get large advances on the project. The total sum: one-and-a-half million dollars!

None of this went to Hughes. Roughly half of it was paid out – and all went into Irving's pocket. Not that it stayed there for long. The spendthrift author splashed out on luxury trips around the world. Wherever he went, he claimed to be keeping secret appointments with Hughes or his associates.

McGraw-Hill constantly fired off telegrams to Irving enquiring about the progress of the book. The author would reply from one five-star hotel or another, stressing the extreme difficulties of his task and Hughes's paranoid insistence on secrecy. Craftily, he maintained the publishers' interest by mailing them sample sections of the manuscript and providing letters supposedly sent to him by Hughes.

The sample chapters contained tantalizing quotations supposedly transcribed from tape-recordings made by Irving with Hughes. Some conversations were said to have taken place over the phone, others in person. The contents of the texts were mainly lies – but lies cleverly intertwined with rumour and half-truth and embroidered with the gleanings of newspaper libraries.

Irving's art-school training came in useful at this stage. For the letters signed by Hughes were in reality written by Irving to himself. The forgeries were so perfect that they fully satisfied the more doubtful sceptics at McGraw-Hill. At one stage, when the publishers became worried about the delay in receiving substantial parts of the manuscripts, they secretly took the Hughes letters to New York's leading handwriting analysts – who confirmed without doubt that they were indeed written by the old man.

Not all of Irving's work was pure fiction, however. The author had a secret source of hitherto unpublished revelations about the recluse. The source was Hughes's former aide, Noah Dietrich, who had made copious notes about his long liaison with the billionaire. Dietrich had been planning to turn this material into a book of his own. But Irving secretly borrowed the aide's notes, copied them and proceeded to lift from them some of the more interesting tit-bits.

McGraw-Hill were well and truly hooked. Tempted by fantastic stories of Hughes's secret World War Two missions, of his friendship with novelist Ernest Hemingway and of his glamorous, globe-trotting life-style, they kept the money pouring in. It arrived by post in the form of cheques made out to Hughes. They were paid into a Swiss bank account but the money did not remain there for long. The account, in the name of H. R. Hughes, had been opened by Edith Irving, using a passport forged by her husband.

Irving must have known that his amazing confidence trick could not last for ever. But when the crash came, it was from the most unexpected direction. By an amazing coincidence, someone else had been plotting a similar scheme to Irving's. A rival publishing house had taken the bait and proudly announced that an authorized biography of Hughes was shortly to be printed.

For a while, panic reigned at McGraw-Hill. The scene of confusion was repeated at the Time-Life organization which had agreed to buy the serialization rights to the Irving book. But the man at the centre of the storm remained as cool as ever. Irving produced a new forged letter from Hughes denouncing the rival book as a fake – and demanding more money for his own.

Raising the price was a master-stroke. McGraw-Hill once again fell for Irving's tale. But for the first time they had to show their own hand and announce the existence of the Irving book.

That sealed the conman's fate. Hughes ordered his lawyers to hold a press conference at which reporters who had followed the astonishing saga of the billionaire recluse were allowed to question Hughes by telephone. The Irving 'autobiography' was denounced, yet the trickster continued his protestations of innocence.

The man who finally shattered Irving's story was Robert Dolan Peloquin, a super-sleuth who had won the title 'Sherlock Holmes of the jet age'. This handsome 6ft 1in American lawyer had spent 16 years in the service of the US Government, taking on the con-men of the Mafia and the sophisticated criminals of the computer world. He was one of Bobby Kennedy's closest aides when the assassinated politician was America's Attorney-General.

Peloquin later left Government service to become president of Intertel, a private international intelligence agency based in Washington DC, with branches throughout the world. Ex-Scotland Yard head of CID Sir Ranulph Bacon joined him on the staff of what has been called 'the world's most formidable private investigating firm'.

It was at Intertel that Peloquin took a call from Chester Davis, lawyer for legendary recluse Hughes, who was alarmed at impending publication of the 'autobiography', and wanted Peloquin to prove the book was a fraud.

This meant knocking holes in publisher McGraw-Hill's claim that Hughes had collaborated with Irving. They based their claim on cheques made out to and endorsed by H. R. Hughes, and deposited in a numbered Swiss bank account. McGraw-Hill said handwriting experts had verified the signatures on them as that of Howard Hughes. But they refused to let Intertel see the cheques for themselves.

The controversy over the book was headline news. And that helped Peloquin get the evidence he needed. An executive of McGraw-Hill went on America's early-morning Today TV programme, brandishing three cheques worth a total of $650,000 and cashed by H. R. Hughes. Peloquin immediately obtained a video tape of the show, froze the frames where the cheques appeared, and had enlargements made of the prints.

It was just possible to see the name of the Zurich bank which had endorsed the payments. Peloquin was on the first available plane.

In Zurich, he was told that H. R. Hughes was a woman. Her description gave him a hunch. He phoned his Washington HQ and asked for a photograph to be wired to him. Four hours later he was back in the bank. The woman in the picture had her hair in a different style, but officials were almost sure she was H. R. Hughes. The picture, of course, was of Irving's wife.

Clifford Irving with his wife Edith and their two sons

Within minutes, the information had been cabled to Chester Davis, who called in the US Attorney in Manhattan. Irving and his wife were arrested.

Irving denied all until the very end. But his lies were finally seen for what they were when internationally famous singer Nina, the beautiful blonde half of the Nina and Frederick folk duo, revealed that at a time when Irving had supposedly been closeted with Howard Hughes, the author had really been with her.

In 1972, Edith Irving, distraught over the stories of her husband's womanizing, was sent to jail for two years in Switzerland. After hearing her sentenced, Irving sobbed: 'I have put my wife in jeopardy. She has suffered terribly. I have heard her cry herself to sleep at night.'

Then he too went down. After cracking and confessing all, Irving was fined

Shock of recognition

Swashbuckling silent screen hero Douglas Fairbanks senior was a great hoaxer. He had a special chair electrically wired to give mild electric shocks to anybody who sat in it. But he came unstuck once when a female fan sat in the chair. He applied the current but she showed no reaction. When he asked if she was feeling all right she explained: 'I thought one always felt like this when meeting a wonderful movie star like you, Mr Fairbanks.'

$10,000 and sentenced to 30 months' jail in the US. He was also ordered to pay back some of the $500,000 he owed McGraw-Hill.

Edith Irving served only 14 months of her sentence and her husband 17 months. But they were never reunited. Edith won a divorce and remarried her husband's former tennis partner. Clifford himself moved down to Mexico with a young woman friend.

There he set about writing another book, legitimately this time. It was a detailed, dramatic account of how he pulled off his $1\frac{1}{2} million superhoax. He needed it to sell well in order to pay off his huge debts. And, ironically, the book was given a huge and topical sales boost soon after with the death in 1975 of the one man whose fabulous wealth had made the hoax of the century possible – Howard Hughes.

Who'll buy a tall story?

The one or two-paragraph items at the foot of newspaper pages are known in the trade as 'fillers'. Over the years they have become something of an art-form to journalists versed in the crafts of cliché, brevity and deadpan humour. Often, to serve these overriding interests, strict truth has come off second best.

The most famous, most imaginative and certainly the most audacious of these filler writers was Louis T. Stone, from Winsted, Connecticut. His career from 1895 to his death in 1933 consisted of paid lying.

It all began when he was working as a young cub reporter and needed $150.

What he actually needed was a story he could sell to the big-city papers. And since there wasn't a story, he decided to invent one.

He filed an account of the Wild Man of Connecticut who roamed through the forests without ever being caught. The story attracted the attention of New York editors, but was quickly spotted as a hoax. Stone, however, had learned a lesson that was to serve him well for the next 38 years.

He realized there was a demand for tall tales and set out to feed the market with gems like these . . .

'I have seen with my own eyes a man in this town – name of Samuel – who had such trouble with the flies buzzing round his old bald head, he painted a spider up there and that sure did scare all them doggoned flies away.'

And this one: 'In the next smallholding to me is a farmer who had a wonderful chicken who laid a red, white and blue egg on July 4th'.

And this: 'We have a cow that is so modest she only allows women to milk her. And another cow down Winsted way produces burning, hot milk, having been grazed on a horseradish patch.'

And this: 'I have seen and heard a cat with a harelip that could whistle Yankee Doodle'.

This too: 'One of the chicken farmers near here always plucks his chickens humanely – with a vacuum cleaner'.

These were all actual stories written by Stone and published as true – but editors just couldn't get enough of them. Many knew they were hoaxes but the readers enjoyed them so much they continued to print them. Certainly the people of Winsted appreciated Stone's efforts. As visitors drove in to the town, billboards greeted them with this sign:

'Winsted, Connecticut, founded in 1779, has been put on the map by the ingenious and queer stories that emanate from this town and which are printed all over the country, thanks to L. T. Stone.'

Stone is also commemorated by a bridge named in his honour. It spans a stream called Sucker Brook.

Lovely leg-pull

An official document circulated in October 1969 by the Ministry of Education and Science stated that West German scientists led by Professor Kitzelbein, had proved that girls with longer and shapelier legs were more intelligent. The report was a hoax pulled by Michael Proctor, First Secretary at the British Embassy in Bonn. And 'Kitzelbein'? It means leg-tickler!

The master-faker who even took Goering for a ride

How many of the treasures of the world's museums and art galleries are genuine and how many fakes will probably never be known. The art forgers are just too clever for most experts.

According to ex-forger David Stein, 'I can open an art catalogue anywhere in the world and recognize my own work.' Master-faker Elmyr de Hory said of the experts: 'They know more about fine words than fine art.' And Hans van Meegeren described them as 'arrogant scum'.

Van Meegeren is recognized as the greatest art forger of all time. But his criminal career was revealed only through the most amazing sequence of events. . . .

After the fall of Nazi Germany in 1945, Hermann Goering's priceless collection of old masters was uncovered at his Berchtesgaden mansion. Most had been looted from churches, galleries and private collections during the German march through Europe. A few, however, had been honestly purchased, and one of these was a painting entitled *Woman Taken in Adultery*. It was signed by Jan Vermeer, the 17th-century Dutch master.

In those first days after the war's end, the hunt was on throughout newly liberated Europe for collaborators. And when it was discovered that Goering's agents had paid £160,000 for the painting from a dealer in Amsterdam, Dutch police thought they had found someone who had been too generous to the Nazis. That someone was van Meegeren.

At that time van Meegeren was a rich nightclub owner who had amassed a small fortune by selling previously undiscovered old masters to major art galleries. Apart from the painting purchased by Goering, he had sold six other works signed by Vermeer to Dutch galleries.

Van Meegeren was arrested and thrown into prison to await trial as a collaborator – a charge which could carry the death sentence. He was interrogated daily for three weeks without changing his story. Then, when he was finally brought to court, he came up with the most astonishing defence.

He said that, far from collaborating with the Nazis, he had actually duped them. He had not sold Goering a Vermeer but a van Meegeren – the old master's work was a fake he had painted himself. And he had sold dozens of others for vast sums around the world.

At first the judge did not believe him. But he gave van Meegeren a chance. Placed under guard in his Amsterdam studio, he was told to paint another

Hans van Meegeren

Vermeer that would fool the experts. He did so – it was titled *Jesus Among the Doctors* – and he was freed.

The master-forger's freedom was, however, short-lived. For as more and more van Meegerens came to light, he was brought to trial again, this time charged with deception. He was jailed for 12 months, but died of a heart attack six weeks later at the age of 57.

What made van Meegeren embark on his career of forgery? Surprisingly, in view of the huge sums his fakes fetched, the motive was not money. Van Meegeren was a relatively successful painter who had his first major exhibition at The Hague when he was 33. It was a sellout, yet the critics slated it.

Foremost among them was a pompous professor, Dr Abraham Bredius, who dismissed van Meegeren's work with contempt. Over the years, the struggling painter's pent-up anger and frustration over Bredius's attacks found an outlet. Van Meegeren began to paint copies of the works of the artist whom Dr Bredius admired most of all: Vermeer.

Throughout 1936 van Meegeren remained in self-imposed exile in a rented villa in France, working on his masterpiece, a perfectly executed 'Vermeer' which he titled *Christ and the Disciples at Emmaus*. He 'aged' the painting 300 years by a process he had painstakingly developed.

In 1937 he put the painting on the market through a Paris lawyer, claiming that it had been in the possession of a Dutch family living in France. The family, so the story went, had fallen on hard times and now needed to sell their heirloom.

Naturally enough, the lawyer first approached Dr Bredius who, as the world's leading authority on Vermeer, could vouch for the painting's authenticity. He had no hesitation in doing so.

But not only did Bredius give his stamp of approval to the painting, he also – to van Meegeren's great delight – claimed the work as his own discovery. Bredius urged that it be bought for £50,000 by Rotterdam's Boyman's Museum. Bredius would often go there to study it – and van Meegeren to gloat over it.

Busting out all over

Perhaps the most prolific forger of sculptures was Giovanni Bastianini who before his death in 1868 turned out terracotta busts by the dozen under contract to an art dealer. They were considered to be perfect examples of Renaissance sculpture, and the Florentine faker's works appeared in museums around the world. There are still two in London's Victoria and Albert Museum.

Disgust at the ignorance of art 'experts' and anger at the dishonesty of dealers prompted another artist, Elmyr de Hory, to go into the faking business.

De Hory, a stateless Hungarian, received the greatest accolade of all when another famous faker, Clifford Irving, the American author later jailed for his forged biography of Howard Hughes, wrote a book about the artist entitling it simply *Fake*.

It was reported that paintings by the stateless Hungarian artist were among millions of dollars' worth of fakes sold to a Texas millionaire. The ensuing scandal made de Hory famous, although he insisted that he had never tried to pass his own work off as that of someone else. He said he had never put a famous signature to one of his own paintings – even when that painting was in the precise style of a sought-after artist.

In 1974, at the age of 60, de Hory was taken from his home on the Spanish island of Ibiza and jailed on Majorca. There was no formal charge, and the artist was out again after four months.

Like so many with his talents, he never disguised his contempt for the international art pundits who 'know more about fine words than fine art'. He claimed he could paint a portrait in 45 minutes, draw a 'Modigliani' in 10 and then immediately knock off a 'Matisse'.

'The dealers, the experts and the critics resent my talent,' he said, 'because they don't want it shown how easily they can be fooled. I have tarnished the infallible image they rely upon for their fortunes.'

Almost as quick on the draw as de Hory, but displaying rather more daring, was another brilliant artist, David Stein, who for a brief but mind-boggling four-year reign was undisputed king of the art forgers.

He was a talented painter in his own right, but the high prices paid in the art world were too great a temptation to resist. Working in watercolours or oils, he recreated the styles of some of the world's best-known artists – living and dead.

The dead gave David Stein no trouble, but the living led to his downfall.

Pressed for time one day, he rushed off three watercolours he had promised a dealer. Working furiously in his New York apartment, the whole fateful operation took just seven hours. At six in the morning he was lying in bed dreaming up ideas for the paintings. At one o'clock the same day he was handing a satisfied art dealer the 'genuine' works of French artist Marc Chagall, each with its own certificate of authentication.

In those seven hours he had treated the paper he used with cold tea to give it the impression of ageing, executed the watercolours, forged the certificates of authentication and Chagall's signature, and had the pictures professionally framed.

The art dealer was delighted when Stein handed over his 'find'. He examined the three forged Chagalls and, without ever suspecting the truth, began

---

Michelangelo's 'Antique'
**There is nothing new about the forgery of art-works.
Michelangelo himself is reputed to have raised much-needed
funds as a struggling young man by selling to a Rome cardinal a
statue of Cupid which the artist had first stained and buried to
age it into an 'antique'.**

---

haggling with Stein over the price. Eventually a cheque for $10,000 changed hands.

The dealer was so proud of his new acquisitions that he determined to show them to someone who had newly arrived in New York – Marc Chagall himself. For, while Stein had busied himself with the forgeries, Chagall had been flying into the city to supervise the installation of two huge murals he had painted in the Metropolitan Opera House.

The dealer had already fixed an appointment to see Chagall and, at their meeting, expected that the great artist would be delighted to see three of his earlier works again. Chagall's reaction at first bewildered then horrified him. 'Diabolical!' said the Frenchman, 'They are not mine.'

Had 31-year-old Stein stuck to Cézannes, Renoirs or Manets, he would have got away with it. As it was, the police came to arrest him that evening. The daredevil forger said afterwards: 'As they arrived at my front door, I left through the back with a glass of Scotch in my hand!'

He made his way to California and it was there that his luck ran out. He was arrested and confessed all. 'If only I had stuck to dead men,' he moaned when he was later indicted on 97 counts of grand larceny and counterfeiting.

While in jail, Stein shared his knowledge of faking with the New York Police Department, helping them create a special art forgery squad. With remission, he served just 16 months and, on his release, he left his three American galleries and half-a-million dollars a year income to return to his native Europe.

This was when the half-French, half-British Stein made his second mistake. He had not realized that the French police also wanted to ask him a few questions. That error cost him another two-and-a-half years in jail.

In the early 1970s, a free man at last, Stein decided to forget the old masters and stick to painting Steins. His fame as a brilliant forger aided his success and he later set up businesses and homes in both London and Paris.

But Stein was still angry at those people he regarded as the real fakers of the art world, the band of ignorant people who claim to be experts.

'A lot of the art world is fake,' he said. 'About two or three hundred of my forgeries are still on the market listed as originals.'

Which is the Mona Lisa?

The rich American collector felt the stirrings of greed. Here he was being offered a work of art that experts agreed was priceless for a knock-down figure of $300,000. It did not matter to him that the men offering the Mona Lisa for sale had stolen it from the Louvre Museum in Paris.

To own such a masterpiece was all he wanted and, who knows, after the fuss had died down maybe his children or his great-grandchildren could one day profit by its sale?

What he never suspected was that the same secret offer had been made to five other Americans. Six Mona Lisas – and not one of them was the real thing!

But the genuine masterpiece *had* been stolen, on August 21, 1911, when three thieves dressed as workmen came out of their overnight basement hiding place and coolly took it off the wall.

The gang consisted of art forger Yves Chaudron, con-man Eduardo de Valfierno, and Italian burglar Vincenzo Perrugia. They knew it was unlikely that the people they tricked would realize that their copy was a fake. Even if they did, they could not go to the police and admit to being part of a shady deal. Their reputations were at stake.

Chaudron and Valfierno had operated a similar scheme in South America. The trick there was to offer to steal a particular painting for a crooked dealer who would then sell it to a client.

Pretending to be art experts, they would ask a gallery owner to allow them to examine the picture. When it was down from the wall, Valfierno would cunningly line the back of the canvas with a forgery of the original painted by Chaudron.

On another visit, with the crooked dealer in tow, the victim would be invited to place his mark on the back of the picture he wanted stolen. Unwittingly, he would be marking the back of the fake. He later received his 'stolen' picture and the gallery owners never knew their part in the con-trick.

If the victim did wonder why the picture still hung on the gallery wall, Chaudron and Valfierno would tell him that a copy of the original had taken its place while the theft was being investigated. Super-salesman Valfierno even produced phoney newspaper cuttings telling of the crime to convince buyers.

The two rogues made enough money to afford the trip to Paris and to live in style there. It was only a matter of time before the Mona Lisa inspired the con-trick of a lifetime.

Perrugia's help was enlisted because, besides being a small-time criminal, he had once worked in the Louvre and knew his way about. He had put the glass in the box that protected Leonardo da Vinci's masterpiece.

Although Chaudron and Valfierno made almost two million dollars from the sale of the forgeries to unsuspecting Americans, they never got the chance to sell the Mona Lisa itself. Perrugia stole it from them and fled to Italy where he clumsily tried to sell it himself.

The gang were uncovered and the Mona Lisa was returned to the Louvre where, under heavy guard, behind a thick glass panel, and surrounded by electronic alarms, it remains today.

The theft of the Mona Lisa was not the first time that the Louvre had been taken for a costly ride. Its worst blunder was revealed in 1903 when a Parisian painter claimed that he was the creator of one of its most treasured possessions – a beautifully intricate golden headdress called the Tiara of Saitaphernes.

The claim was untrue. The tiara was a fake, sure enough. But the man who had made it was not the Parisian painter. Its creator was a Russian goldsmith, Israel Rouchomowsky.

Rouchomowsky did not want the false claimant to take credit for his work, so he travelled to Paris to put the record straight. The administrators of the Louvre continued to deny that the tiara was a fake until the old Russian produced the original designs he had drawn for the headdress eight years earlier – and, to rub salt in the wounds, began working on a new tiara, as intricate in every detail as that in the Louvre.

The faker famous for his 'Sexton Blakes'

Brilliant faker Tom Keating rocked the art world he despised with his amazing imitations of the works of great masters. In 1979, at the age of 62, he went on trial at the Old Bailey for forgery. But all the charges were dropped when his health deteriorated.

Keating, a big bearded ex-naval stoker, called his fakes, in Cockney rhyming slang, 'Sexton Blakes'. At first he painted them to get even with the dealers who had, he reckoned, exploited him.

As a young man, he had lived in a damp prefab with his wife and two children, and was paid £5 a time to copy other artists. He angrily quit the job when he found his paintings on sale in galleries for £500.

'Those dealers are just East End blokes in West End suits,' he said. 'They

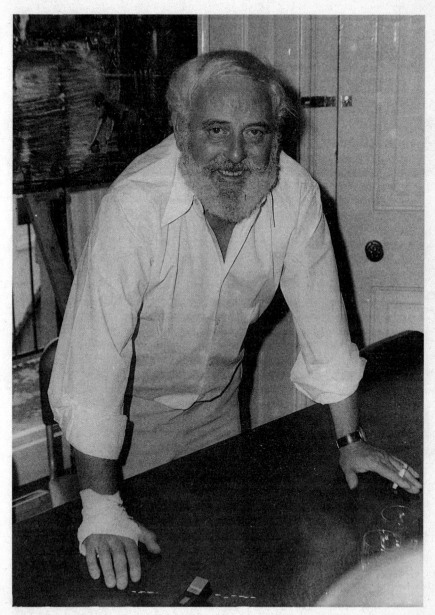

Artist, Tom Keating

Fake Madonna

America's Cleveland Museum of Art had to remove from display one of its most prized possessions, a wooden Madonna and Child, supposedly carved in Italy in the 13th century. In fact, it was carved around 1920 by an Italian art restorer, Alceo Dossena. His fake was only discovered when in 1927 the sculpture was X-rayed and modern nails were found to be embedded in the wood.

The museum put the Madonna and Child in its basement and looked around for other works to replace it. Three weeks later it bought a marble statue of Athena for $120,000. It, too, was a Dossena fake.

don't give a damn about the paintings. All they're after is the profit.'

In the 1950s his marriage broke up and he went to Scotland to restore murals. While he was there he began imitating the works of other painters and sending them to auction.

He returned to London in 1960 for his most important commission – restoring the pictures in Marlborough House which had been empty since the death of Queen Mary in 1953.

One day he met Queen Elizabeth while carrying out the restoration of a giant painting by Laguerre of the Duke of Marlborough.

In his book, *The Fake's Progress*, Keating recalls: 'The Queen came up the stairs and gazed at it in astonishment. She turned to me and mentioned that she had run up and down the stairs hundreds of times as a little girl but had not been aware these beautiful pictures were on the wall. "Well they are madam," I said. "And there's a lot more under the black varnish on the other walls."'

Then, according to Keating, the Queen watched him use a solvent to clean a section of the painting.

The work at Marlborough House was an isolated job for hard-up Keating. Most of his time would be spent turning out his 'Sexton Blakes' by the score, giving most of them away but selling others through auction rooms.

In 1963 he read a book on the 19th-century artist Samuel Palmer and became captivated by him. He scoured the art galleries looking for examples of Palmer's work to copy. At the Tate, said Keating, he touched one 'and a strange sensation went through me like an electric shock'.

Keating was a perfectionist. He was always careful about selecting the right paper or canvas. And he claimed that the spirit of Palmer would guide his hand.

'I'd sit in my little sketching room waiting for it to happen,' he explained. 'I have never drawn a sheep from life but then Palmer's sheep would begin to appear on the paper. Then Palmer's *Valley of Vision Watched Over by the Good Shepherd in the Shadow of Shoreham Church*. With Sam's permission I sometimes signed them with his own name, but they were his, not mine. It was his hand that guided the pen.'

It was also in 1963 that Keating met Jane Kelly, a pretty convent-educated schoolgirl busy studying for her exams. In Bohemian coffee bars, she and her friends would cluster round the painter, treating him almost as a guru.

Jane was 17, Keating 46. Yet, after the death of her boy-friend in a road accident, they fell in love – and the impressionable teenager became the painter's mistress. They moved to historic Wattisfield Hall in Suffolk, where Jane restored pictures and Keating embarked on a prodigious output of fakes.

When, at the Old Bailey in 1979, Keating was shown his most famous fake – a sepia, ink-wash of *Sepham Barn* sold for £9,400 as a genuine Palmer – he told the jury: 'I am ashamed of this piece of work.'

He had no recollection of painting it, he said. It had, however, been done using modern materials, the main figure of a shepherd was 'un-Palmerish' and the flock of sheep 'unsheep-like'. It was the sort of painting, he confessed, that he would normally have burnt or thrown away.

Looking at another work subsequently sold for £2,550, Keating appeared bemused and said: 'That must have taken me about half an hour. It's just a doodle. It has the ingredients of Palmer but not his technical ability of aesthetic appeal'.

The 'doodle' was of a barn at Shoreham, which had been sold at a country auction for £35. It was later sold by a London gallery to Bedford Museum for £2,550 after restoration work by the National Gallery.

Bemusing the Met

In 1918 the New York Metropolitan Museum of Art paid $40,000 for the 7-ft statue of an Etruscan warrior which had supposedly been buried since pre-Roman days. One arm of the warrior was missing, as was the thumb of his other hand.

In 1960 Alfredo Fioravanti confessed to the museum that he was one of six men who had created the statue between them 50 years earlier. He produced the warrior's missing thumb to prove it. The thumb fitted perfectly.

In 1975 the same museum had to withdraw from display a beautiful 'Greek' bronze horse when it was shown to be a fake. The horse had been one of the museum's most popular attractions.

After the sale of *Sepham Barn*, Keating and Jane went to live in Tenerife. There, Jane met a Canadian with whom she fell in love and whom she later married. The nine-year affair between Jane and Keating was over. They met again seven years later – when Jane gave evidence at the Old Bailey about Keating's famous fakes. The scandal, which ruined many reputations in the art world, broke after an expert had written in *The Times* suggesting *Sepham Barn* was not genuine.

By Keating's own rough count, no fewer than 2,500 of his fake pictures are hanging in galleries or on collectors' walls. No one will ever know which are fakes and which are old masters. Not even Tom Keating who, after his trial was stopped, continued turning out his paintings – at a price.

Because of his notoriety, Keating's works became highly prized. 'Suddenly everyone wants to own a Keating,' said one gallery owner. 'Prices have doubled in a month. His paintings are going round the world.'

Keating was offered a £250,000 contract from one London gallery and a £30,000 commission for a single portrait. He turned both down.

'I have enough work to make me rich beyond my wildest dreams,' he said. 'But I've met many millionaires and they have all been miserable. All I have ever wanted to do is to paint. I would give all the damn things away if I could afford to. Painting is God's gift, not mine, and it should be used to bring pleasure.'

At the height of his fame, a television film was made about the master-faker's life and work. Director Rex Bloomstein got to know him well. He said of Keating:

'He was a very emotional man. When painting, he would cry and shiver. He said he felt the artist come down and guide his hand. he was the most fascinating, complex person I have ever met.'

Crowning jest

In 1902 hundreds of upper-crust Americans received invitations to the Coronation of Edward VII and Queen Alexandra of England. Attached to each invitation was a set of instructions about the proper attire for the Coronation. Wealthy Americans were asked to turn up in costumes typifying the origins of their titles. Coal barons might wear miners' helmets, judges might carry six-shooters, and railway tycoons might sport guards' whistles. The invitations were, of course, a hoax. But they were cleverly adapted facsimiles of the genuine articles.

The pitfalls of literature

Two of the most famous forgers of all time were teenagers. Both lived in the 18th century, both forged literature, and their names were Thomas Chatterton and William Henry Ireland.

Chatterton became known as 'the Marvellous Boy'. Before he was 10 he had taught himself how to write in Gothic characters by copying from an old Bible. In 1765, when only 12, he started producing ancient poems which he claimed he had found in an old chest in the local church. He said they had been written by a priest named Thomas Rowley, possibly around Chaucer's time – 400 years earlier.

Not only did these odes convince scholars of their antiquity but they also received some fine critical acclaim. Spurred by his success, Thomas left his native Bristol for London. But the London experts were not fooled so easily and declared his works to be forgeries.

Although he had a minor success with his own poems and political satires, Thomas Chatterton's career was soon in ruins and at 17 he took his own life.

In his will, he left 'all the young ladies my letters and poems. I leave my mother and sister to the protection of my friends if I have any.'

Chatterton was later recognized to have been a budding genius. He became an inspiration to later poets such as Wordsworth, Shelley and Coleridge. He was immortalized in a painting by Henry Wallis and is the only forger to have had an entire opera written about him – Leoncavallo's *Chatterton*.

The other teenage forger of that time was William Henry Ireland who, although not so talented, also made the stage – with a Shakespearian production which he wrote himself.

William had started early by handing over spurious Shakespearian manuscripts and artefacts to his father, a London bookseller and Shakespeare enthusiast. William claimed that while working as a solicitor's clerk, a mysterious gentleman had entrusted all the documents into his safe-keeping. These he showed his father, who showed them to friends – and the news of the Shakespeare discoveries spread like wildfire.

What began as a jape rapidly turned into an industry. The young Ireland produced a land deed and other private papers of William Shakespeare. Then he got bolder and produced original transcripts of parts of *King Lear* and extracts from *Hamlet*. These were so convincing that even the diarist and biographer James Boswell paid homage. He said: 'I now kiss the invaluable relics of our bard to thank God that I have lived to see them.'

With this sort of success under his belt, Ireland really went to town. At the age

Thomas Chatterton

of 17, he 'discovered' a brand new Shakespearean play which no one had seen before. He called it *Vortigern*.

The play was produced at the Drury Lane Theatre on April 2, 1796. The actor-manager John Kemble, who was to play the lead, had his doubts about the authenticity of the piece and suggested that it would have been more appropriate to open the play a day earlier on April Fool's Day. But although the play did open on April 2, Kemble got the last laugh. In Act Five there was a speech which contained a line that brought the house down. . . .

'And when this solemn mockery is ended. . . .'

The audience hooted the rest of the play off the stage. The first performance of *Vortigern* was also its last and the game was up for Ireland. The rest of his forgeries were detected and the teenager confessed to everything – although his old father could never bring himself to believe that his treasured possessions were all fakes.

The bullet that found its mark 20 years late

Henry Ziegland thought he was a dead man. Standing before him was an angry young man, gun in hand, telling him that he was about to kill him. The gunman was the brother of Ziegland's ex-girlfriend, who had just committed suicide after being jilted. The brother was out for revenge.

The gunman pulled the trigger. The bullet grazed Ziegland's face and buried itself in a tree. Ziegland fell to the ground and stayed still, as the brother, thinking he had accomplished his mission, turned the gun on himself and blew his brains out.

The murder that never was occurred in Honey Grove, Texas, in 1893. Over the next 20 years, Ziegland put the incident from his mind. One day in 1913 he decided to fell the tree on his land under which the shooting had occurred. It was a tough job, so he used dynamite.

He drilled a hole in the tree trunk, filled it with explosive and set the fuse. The explosion blasted fragments in all directions – and sent the old bullet through Henry Ziegland's head, killing him instantly.

Chapter
Four

Brigands and Outlaws

'The Devil, depend upon it, can sometimes do a very gentlemanly thing'
Robert Louis Stevenson

The most wanted men in the West

What was the truth about the Wild West? Our ideas tend to have been formed by characters like Tom Mix, Gene Autry, the Lone Ranger and Roy Rogers. Screen idols through the years have portrayed the cowboy as a slick, good-looking, gun-totin', lariat-twirling goodie in a white hat, or scheming, scowling baddie in a black hat.

Hollywood took the names of men like Billy the Kid, Jesse James and Butch Cassidy and turned them into heroes. But few of the folk who lived and died in the 19th-century West would have agreed. . . .

Baptist minister's son Jesse Woodson James strolled into the Clay County Savings Bank in Liberty, Missouri, on February 13, 1866, and took the liberty of relieving cashier Mr Greenup Bird of $60,000.

It was the start of a bloodthirsty war that the James boys and their daring cousins, the Youngers, waged throughout Kansas and Missouri. They got away with gunning-down train guards and bank tellers because nobody knew what the villains looked like – since none of them ever had his photograph taken.

Jesse would openly stroll around Nashville and Kansas City, calling himself Mr Howard, and on one occasion even bought a drink for a Pinkerton Agency detective searching for him.

Detective Bligh confided to 'Mr Howard' that his last wish would be to confront Jesse James. Later James sent him a note: 'Go ahead and die. You've seen Jesse James.'

Jesse loved playing to the crowd. On one occasion during a Missouri train hold-up, he personally presented the guard with his latest press cuttings.

The day Jesse and his boys slipped up was when they tried to rob the First National Bank in Northfield, Minnesota. The townsfolk had been tipped off that the gang were on their way, and as they arrived in town they were met with a hail of bullets, grapeshot and even bricks. Two of the gang were blown to pieces, three Younger brothers were captured, but Jesse got away.

The man who finally put paid to Jesse James was a gunslinger named Bob Ford, who joined the gang after secretly agreeing with the authorities to assassinate James for a free pardon and part of the reward money.

On April 3, 1882, Jesse, then aged 35, got up to straighten his favourite 'Home, Sweet Home' picture on the wall of his bunkhouse abode. Ford blew off the back of his head, and his brains scattered across the floor.

The owner of the house where Jesse died, at St Joseph, Missouri, chopped up

The only authentic portrait of Billy the Kid

the floor and sold the blood-stained wood-shavings for five dollars a time.

The James gang's greatest partners in crime were the Younger family. Cole Younger, then 28, first teamed up with Jesse's gang in Logan County, Kentucky, in 1868, to rob the local bank.

Cole had already met Jesse as one of Quantrill's Raiders at the massacre of Lawrence, Kansas, where, in one of the most unparalleled acts of savagery in the West, 150 men and boys were shot by William Quantrill's Confederate guerillas.

Cole had a passionate love affair with Myra Belle Shirley, the 18-year-old daughter of a Dallas horse-breeder. After two disastrous marriages, she went on to achieve notoriety as Belle Starr.

The other Younger brothers – Bob, 18, Jim, 26, and John, 28 – later joined Cole in the James gang. John died from a Pinkerton bullet and the surviving three were captured and jailed for life after the Northfield, Missouri shoot-out.

Butch Cassidy and the Sundance Kid were turned into posthumous superstars thanks to one successful film. In real life, neither were heroes – although a cut above some of the other crooks of the age.

Butch Cassidy was born Robert Leroy Parker in 1867 in Beaver, Utah, but later changed his name as a token of respect to his idol Mike Cassidy who taught him the arts of rustling and horse stealing.

In his youth, Butch was involved in everything from petty larceny to train and bank hold-ups. But it wasn't until he was released from Rawlings Penitentiary, Wyoming, that he decided to get his own gang together. They soon became known as the Wild Bunch.

Legend has it that Butch, eulogized by contemporary posters as a cheery, affable character, never shot directly at a man. When pursued by a posse he would always fire at the horses.

Trains were the speciality of Butch and his Wild Bunch. One day they scooped $30,000 from a Union Pacific express by detaching the last car and blowing it and the safe inside to smithereens. They followed this success with three more train raids until Pinkerton agents got on the gang's trail.

The Pinkertons and the railroad's own crime fighters forced the gang to seek refuge in South America. Around 1909 (some say in Bolivia, others in Uruguay), Butch and his chief cohort in crime, Harry 'Sundance' Longbaugh, either committed suicide or were shot dead in a battle with troops.

Harry Longbaugh had got his nickname when, as a boy, he served 18 months in jail at Sundance, Cook County, Wyoming, for horse stealing. Thereafter, he called himself the Sundance Kid.

The Kid had no raindrops falling on his head – only 'wanted' posters. In late 1901, Sundance and his lady love, Etta Place, sailed for Buenos Aires after being run out of the US by the Pinkertons.

The Wild Bunch. Butch Cassidy is seated on the right and the Sundance Kid on the left.

He continued robbing banks and trains, managing to keep one step ahead of the law by hiding out among local Indians, until his death alongside Butch Cassidy.

The most famous gunfighter of the West was a soft-spoken, agreeable young man named William Bonney, better known as Billy the Kid. Believed to have been born in New York, he moved west with his family and became a cowboy in Lincoln County, New Mexico. There he worked for an English ranch owner John Tunstall, who befriended him.

In March 1878, two killers riding with the posse of corrupt Sheriff Brady of Pecos blasted Tunstall to death. When Bonney, then aged 19, heard of his benefactor's death, he grabbed a pair of Colt 44s and went looking for the two killers.

Billy found them and shot them dead. Then, with a price on his head, he teamed up with a gang whose members put paid to Sheriff Brady.

By now, Bonney's fame was spreading. People began talking about a gunslinger named Billy the Kid.

THE WORLD'S GREATEST CROOKS AND CONMEN

State Governor Wallace tried to con Billy into giving himself up. Wallace hired the Kid's one-time friend, Pat Garrett, who persuaded Billy to testify at an inquiry into gang warfare in Lincoln County in exchange for a light sentence.

The Kid walked smack into the trap – but shot his way to freedom. Unknown to Billy, Garrett was made Sheriff of Lincoln County in recognition of his treachery.

Still trading on their old friendship, Garrett guessed that eventually the Kid would head towards the hideout of a mutual friend, Pete Maxwell.

Garrett got there first, urging Maxwell to persuade Billy to surrender. But as they were talking, Billy walked in – straight into two slugs from Garrett's Colt.

Billy the Kid, 21, sprawled dead with 19 notches on his gun. But he could never add up. He had actually killed 21 people in less than two years to avenge his friend and earn himself a place in American legend.

The Wild West is packed with stories of vicious outlaws. But one robber who stood apart was Black Bart. He was always courteous, never hurt anybody and stole only from the treasure box and mailbags, never from the passengers.

Bart's first hold-up was on a blazing hot day in 1875 when he stopped a Wells Fargo stagecoach near Sonora, California. As the horses struggled up a hill, a strange armed man jumped out from the bushes. He wore a flour sack on his head, with holes cut out for the eyes, and a long, white coat.

He ordered the driver to throw down the box and mailbags, and he shouted to his hidden accomplices to shoot if anyone offered resistance. The driver saw six guns poking out from the bushes. They were all trained on the stagecoach.

What followed that day has passed into Western folklore. For when a petrified woman passenger threw her purse at Bart's feet, he calmly picked it up. With a gracious bow, he returned the purse and said he was interested only in the treasure box and mailbags. Not passengers' money or valuables. The strange robber took his loot and told the driver to continue his journey.

For several years, Black Bart robbed in his cavalier manner. His reputation and courteous ways became the talk of California. And he never earned more than £250 from each of his stagecoach robberies, since most gold and valuables were by then transported by train

The man given the task of nailing Black Bart was Jim Hume, Wells Fargo's chief detective.

He soon realized that Bart was cunning and resourceful. When he visited the scene of that first robbery, Bart's 'gang' were still there – six sticks poking through the bushes.

Hume learned little about Bart. He left no clues, his trail just petered out and he seemed to walk everywhere rather than ride.

Bart became bolder and even left Hume his name and a poem at the scene of

Charles E. Bolton, alias Black Bart

one of his crimes. Then Black Bart began to slip up.

After a series of hold-ups, Hume visited houses in the area and learned that a grey-haired, hitch-hiking stranger with a grey beard, white moustache and two missing front teeth had stopped to have dinner. A picture of the hooded raider was at last emerging.

A laundry mark on a handkerchief finally led to Black Bart's capture in 1882. The thief managed to escape unharmed when he was interrupted by a young gunman as he was about to rob a coach. But he blundered by leaving his sleeping-roll and his handkerchief.

Jim Hume had no trouble tracing the laundry mark to a San Francisco laundry – and that led him to a Mr Bolton. He was an elderly man, softly spoken, with grey hair, grey beard, white moustache and two missing front teeth.

Mr Bolton explained his long absences from home by saying that he had to make frequent visits to his mine. But there was no mine, and Jim Hume knew he had his man when Black Bart's clothes were found at Bolton's home.

Black Bart was arrested and, courteous to the end, returned much of the money taken on his raids. For their part, Wells Fargo made charges only on one hold-up and forgot about the others.

By now, the gentlemanly thief had become a popular hero. The judge must have had a soft spot for him, too. He was jailed for six years. It could have been worse.

Black Bart Bolton may have been one of the last stagecoach robbers – but he is remembered first and foremost as the outlaw who wouldn't hurt a fly.

Worst of the 'goodies'!

If the baddies of the Wild West were bad, the goodies were often worse! The men whose job it was to dispense law and order were frequently as lawless as their criminal quarry.

In the West, theatrical farces were put on in saloons and dance halls. But perhaps the most farcical scenarios were those staged by the local judges: and the most unorthodox of all these dispensers of justice was Judge Roy Bean.

A former Civil War guerilla, Judge Roy was a gambler, saloon-keeper and one-time smuggler who got the judge's job in Vinegaroon, Texas, at the age of

Judge Roy Bean

56 because he had picked up a smattering of law while running a construction camp saloon. Mindful of his background, he would regularly stop trials to serve liquor to counsel, jury and defendants, and play a couple of hands of poker before resuming.

He made his own laws and meted out his own fines, most of which he pocketed. He once doubled as a coroner after a worker had fallen 300 ft to his death. Bean did not think the coroner's five-dollar fee was enough, so he searched the body and found $40 and a revolver.

Said Judge Roy: 'I find this corpse guilty of carrying a concealed weapon – and I fine it $40.'

It is doubtful whether a twerp like Wyatt Earp ever became Marshal of Dodge City or even Tombstone. Chroniclers of the West said he brought peace and prosperity to the two frontier towns. But the myth was hatched by writer Stuart Lake, who sold a story to the *Saturday Evening Post*, praising 'lawman' Earp.

Earp, born in 1848, was only briefly a lawman. He took the job of Marshal of Lamar, Missouri, but soon decided that hunting buffalo in Kansas was more fun.

He became a card-sharp and worked a double-act in Wichita – as a gambler by night and a policeman by day. After being thrown out of town, he became assistant Marshal of Dodge City, a member of the local church, an alcoholic and womanizer. His two great boozing buddies were Ford County Sheriff Bat Masterson and James Henry 'Doc' Holliday.

The people of Dodge became fed up with Earp's activities and fired him. In 1879, Wyatt, his brothers and Doc Holliday arrived in Tombstone, Arizona, and set out to make their fortunes by fair means or foul.

Wyatt worked for Wells Fargo before being offered the job of keeping the peace in one of the town's gambling dens. His cronies were installed as croupiers, his brother Virgil became acting Marshal (after the murder of the unfortunte incumbent) and the Earp fortunes prospered.

In 1881 the Tombstone stage was held up. Rumour had it that Earp, Holliday and Masterson had masterminded the robbery with the help of the Clanton Gang. Nevertheless, it was the Earp brothers and Masterson who led the unsuccessful posse in its search for the raiders!

When, later that year, he had his shoot-out with the Clantons at the famous OK Corral, Earp made sure that nobody was left alive to put the finger on him.

Earp soon left Tombstone and, after running saloons in Alaska and Nevada, died in Los Angeles in 1929 at the age of 80. Stuart Lake's biography immortalizing the 'noble lawman' was published after his death – and was denounced by relatives as 'a pack of lies'.

But Wyatt Earp was a paragon of virtue compared with his friend John 'Doc'

Wyatt Earp

Holliday. Holliday was an alcoholic, an inveterate gambler, was tubercular and a walking skeleton with a dangerous temper. He would kill at the slightest provocation.

He originally came west from Baltimore, with qualifications as a dentist, because the climate was better for his health. He did other people's health no good at all. Holliday had gunned down 14 men even before the famous OK Corral shoot-out. Doc died in 1887, a victim of raging consumption. He was just 39.

In their quest for a character who really symbolized law and order in the cow towns, Wild West chroniclers hit upon one James Butler Hickok.

Long-haired, cold-eyed, Wild Bill Hickok was a Union scout in the Civil War who became a professional gambler and once shot dead a dealer who had been producing aces from the bottom of the deck.

Stories about his gunfighting prowess – most of which he had dreamed up himself – won him the job of Marshal of Abilene, Kansas. But he was sacked after shooting wildly at a party of roistering drunks and killing one of his own deputies instead.

Hickok went on a wild spree of boozing, gambling and whoring. In 1876, he was shot in the back during a poker game. He too was 39 when he died.

In his heyday, Wild Bill Hickok had teamed up with Buffalo Bill in his famous travelling stage show. The two men had a lot in common. Both were liars and both liked the bottle.

Buffalo Bill (real name William Frederick Cody, born Iowa, 1846) was a Pony Express rider, buffalo shooter, Indian fighter, cowpuncher, intrepid scout and incredible boaster.

He was encouraged in this latter practice by the wildly exaggerated claims of author Ned Buntline who churned out 121 dime novels supposedly based on the life of Buffalo Bill.

One boozy afternoon in North Platte, Nebraska, overhearing that no festivities had been planned for the forthcoming July 4 celebrations, Cody spontaneously organized a local talent contest, advertising for cowboys to display their skills.

He expected a hundred. Over a thousand cowboys turned up. That was the start of the famous Buffalo Bill Wild West Show which toured the West for 30 years and was even seen on Broadway and across Europe. Queen Victoria was in the audience when it toured Britain.

Like all good hard-living, hard-drinking entrepreneurs, Buffalo Bill Cody died in 1917 – broke.

The ugliest gals in the West

Beauty, grace, fresh-faced femininity . . . the famous gals of the old West had none of these. Despite their portrayal on cinema screens as glamorous, gun-totin' ladies, these women were often worse than their violent menfolk. And from the photographs that have been passed down to us, we know that the one thing they lacked was good looks. In fact, most of them were downright ugly!

CROOKS AND COMMEN

Calamity Jane in 1880

Belle Starr and Indian Blue Duck

They had names like Calamity Jane, Belle Starr, Dutch Annie, Blonde Marie, Madame Moustache, China Mary and Big Nose Kate.

Often they would just as soon shoot you as take you to bed. And for 30 roistering years in the mid-1800s they drank, fought, shot and loved their way into Western legend.

Calamity Jane (born Martha Jane Caaery) got her nickname because so many of her lovers wound up on Boot Hill. She was a drunkard, chewed tobacco, swore like a cavalry trooper and packed an equally hefty punch.

She became a mule-skinner, an army scout, served under General Custer and fell in love with Wild Bill Hickok, near whose grave she was buried in 1903. Calamity was also the biggest liar in the West.

Belle Starr was a notorious outlaw who loved and bore a child to Cole Younger and who rode with Jesse James. Born Myra Belle Shirley, she married an Oklahoma Indian named Sam Starr and was sent to jail with him for horse-stealing.

She also had affairs with bandit Jim Reed (shot dead), a man named John Middleton (shot dead by Sam Starr), Indian desperado Blue Duck (also shot by Starr) and another Indian, Jim July, who survived her. Sam Starr himself was shot dead in a gunfight. And Belle was shot in the back while out riding in 1889. She was 41.

Poker Alice was really Alice Ivers, daughter of an English schoolteacher, who married a card-sharp mining engineer. She won her nickname by spending more time at the gaming tables than at home.

She smoked large cigars, wore outlandish, expensive clothes and, after the death of her husband, opened a brothel. She was as fast with a gun as she was with the cards, and in her long career she shot dead at least two men.

She died virtually penniless in 1930 at the age of 79.

Dutch Annie, Blonde Marie, Madame Moustache and China Mary were all brothel queens, vying with each other for the favours of the hard-drinking, hard-loving frontiersman. They had their counterparts in every cattle-town from the Dakotas to New Mexico.

Big Nose Kate, born Kate Fisher, was a dance-hall girl who attached herself to the Earp gang and became girl-friend to 'Doc' Holliday somewhere between Dodge City and Tombstone.

Holliday must have been shortsighted as well as an alcoholic for Kate was the ugliest of the lot. But she did establish Tombstone's first dance-hall in a specially built marquee.

Pauline Cushman was one of the sexiest, wildest, man-destroying predators in the West. A one-time actress turned bar-fly, she would goad men into gunfights and then sleep with the winner. In San Francisco music-halls, men would go wild as she came on stage, firing six-guns into the ceiling.

Dick Turpin, 'king of the road'

Stand and deliver!' Travellers on the muddy, rutted, bumpy roads of Britain trembled at that cry for almost 200 years. But these travellers, although in peril of losing their purses, were seldom in fear of their lives. For many of the highwaymen who haunted the main routes through England between the early 1600s, until 1815, when a permanent police force was introduced, were gallant men. Rather than common thieves, they were often toasted as gentlemen who happened to have fallen on hard times.

Over the years an aura of glamour surrounded those dashing, charming perfectly behaved brigands of the night. They were heroes of literature and even of song – as in the most popular opera of the 18th century, *The Beggar's Opera*. But no highwayman was made more famous than the young man known as the 'King of the Road' – Dick Turpin.

Turpin was born in 1705 at the Bell Inn in the village of Hempstead, Essex. The inn, since renamed the Rose and Crown, was owned by his father, an ex-butcher. At 16, Dick was apprenticed to a London butcher, but the move to the big city gave him extravagant tastes and at night he became a footpad to eke out his modest income.

Completing his apprenticeship, young Turpin returned to Essex, married and set up in business as a butcher on his own account. He wasn't successful, however, and again he turned to crime. In 1729 he was caught selling stolen carcasses and he went on the run. He became a housebreaker, a cattle thief, a smuggler, a deer poacher in Epping Forest – and eventually a highwayman.

In 1736 one of the best-known criminal partnerships of all time was forged. Turpin was 'working' the Cambridge road out of London when he saw an immaculately dressed horseman approaching. 'Stand and deliver,' demanded Turpin. But the inexperienced highwayman received in reply only a laugh of derision from his intended victim, who was none other than the most famous brigand of the day, Robert King, known as the 'Gentleman Highwayman'.

Their partnership ended a year later in a shoot-out with London police. Turpin had earlier held up a horse dealer and stolen his prize racehorse. It was a reckless act as the horse would certainly be recognized. Sure enough, Turpin was spotted riding through the city. In an ambush, King was shot by the police, King's brother was accidentally shot by Turpin, and the highwayman fled.

He fled north, to Cambridge, Lincoln and finally Yorkshire, all the time making a living by sheep stealing. In Yorkshire, under the name of John Palmer, he would hunt with the local hounds, dine with the local gentry, and

CROOKS AND CONMEN

Dick Turpin

dally with the local ladies, in between 'business trips'.

After one particularly wild night of revelry near York, Turpin began firing off his pistols in the street and ended up in jail while magistrates investigated his recent misdemeanours. Desperate that his real identity should not be discovered, he wrote to his brother back home at the Bell Inn, Hempstead.

Dear Brother,

I am sorry to acquaint you that I am now under confinement in York Castle for horse stealing. If I could procure an evidence from London to give me a character, that would go a great way towards my being acquitted. I had not been long in this country before my being apprehended, so that it would pass off the readier. For Heaven's sake, dear brother, do not neglect me. You will know what I mean when I say

I am yours
John Palmer.

Unfortunately for Turpin, the postmaster at Hempstead was Dick's old schoolmaster, James Smith, the man who had taught the young Turpin to read and write. Incredibly, he recognized his ex-pupil's handwriting and reported the matter. Smith was sent to York to identify Turpin and received £200 reward.

Dick admitted all, was tried and inevitably sentenced to be hanged. While awaiting execution he sat chained in leg-irons in York Prison cheerfully welcoming a steady flow of admiring visitors.

On the morning of April 7, 1739, Turpin was led through crowds of onlookers to the gallows on what is now York racecourse. 'All the way', according to a witness, 'he bowed repeatedly and with the most astonishing indifference and intrepidity.'

Standing undaunted, head held high, Dick Turpin hurled himself from the platform to ensure a brave but speedy end to his daredevil days.

But what of the most famous story of all about the dashing highwayman? According to tradition, books, films and television, Turpin once rode his horse Black Bess non-stop 200 miles from London to York to avoid capture. It is a romantic tale . . . but pure fiction.

Winning ways

In 1928, Liberian President Charles King put himself up for re-election. He was returned with an officially stated majority of 600,000 votes. King's opponent in the poll, Thomas Faulkner, later claimed that the election has been rigged. When asked to substantiate his allegations, Faulkner pointed out that it was difficult to win a 600,000 majority when the total eligible electorate was less than 15,000.

The most heroic legend in the history of crime

He was a criminal, a violent outlaw and highway robber who, with a band of common thieves, plundered the traffic of the king's highway. Yet he is the most enduring hero of his age. His name: Robin Hood.

It is a name that, against all the odds, has survived 600 years. Detail about him has always been scant. His nefarious activities, if true, were in any case minor. And he was not immortalized in any great literature. The illiterate peasantry of the Middle Ages passed on his name, his fame and his supposed deeds by word of mouth from one generation to another – in ballads and fireside stories. As a result, an obscure criminal, with no place in history, acquired international fame. He is the subject of films and television series which owe more to scriptwriters' imagination than to historical research.

How much of the Robin Hood legend is true? Historians over the centuries have debated the issue, challenging his adventures, and disagreeing on the vital question as to whether there even was an outlaw called Robin Hood in Sherwood Forest in the late 13th or early 14th century.

Some believe that the stories of the sprite-like hero may be connected with a mythological pagan woodland spirit. Robin was a name often given to fairies, and green is the supposed colour of the wood spirits – Robin Hood is always depicted as wearing green. There is also a theory that the outlaw was the incarnation of one of the characters depicted in ancient May Day ceremonies. 'Maid Marian' may also have appeared in the celebrations, as Queen of the May.

However, records do show that in the 13th and 14th centuries there lived in Wakefield, Yorkshire a real Robin Hood who may have been the legendary outlaw. This Robin, christened Robert Hood, was born in about 1290. His father, Adam Hood, was a forester in the service of John, Earl Warenne, lord of the manor of Wakefield. The surname in old court documents is variously spelt Hod, Hode and Hood.

On January 25, 1316, Robin Hood's 'handmaid' is recorded as having been brought before a court for taking dry wood and 'vert' from the 'old oak'. Vert is the old English term for trees which provide shelter and food for deer. She was fined twopence. Other court records for the year 1316 show that Robin Hood and his wife Matilda paid two shillings 'for leave to take one piece of land of the lord's waste' to build a five-roomed house.

In 1322, Robin's landlord – at this time, Thomas, Earl of Lancaster – called his tenants to arms in rebellion against King Edward II. A tenant had no choice but to obey his lord implicitly, and Robin Hood followed the earl into battle as an archer. The revolt was crushed. Lancaster was tried for treason and beheaded. His estates were forfeited to the king and his followers were outlawed.

Robin Hood fled into Barnsdale Forest, which at that time covered about 30 square miles of Yorkshire and was linked to Nottinghamshire's Sherwood Forest, with an area of 25 square miles. The forests were traversed by the Roman-built Great North Road, with its rich pickings for robbers. And so the legend of Robin Hood was born.

One of Robin's supposed escapades along this highway concerns the haughty Bishop of Hereford, who was travelling to York when he came across the outlaw leader and some of his companions roasting venison. Taking them for peasants, and infuriated by the flagrant breach of forest laws, the bishop demanded an explanation. The outlaws calmly told him that they were about to dine. The bishop ordered his attendants to seize them.

The outlaws begged for mercy but the bishop swore that he would show them none. So Robin blew on his horn, and the unhappy bishop found himself surrounded by archers in Lincoln green. They took him prisoner, with all his company, and demanded a ransom, amusing themselves by making him dance a jig around a large oak tree. The tree is no longer there but the ground on which it stood is known as Bishop's Tree Root.

Several other oak trees in Barnsdale and Sherwood are associated with Robin Hood and his band. Centre Tree, half way between Thoresby and Welbeck, is said to be the marker from which Robin Hood's network of secret routes stretched through the forest. But the most famous tree is Major Oak, at Birkland. It is reputedly a thousand years old and has a girth of about 29 feet. Alfred, Lord Tennyson visited this oak in the 19th century and in his poem 'The Foresters', has Little John referring to it as '. . . that oak where twelve men can stand inside nor touch each other'.

Among the stories passed down the centuries about Robin Hood's prowess is that of a visit he made with his closest friend, Little John, to Whitby Abbey. The abbot asked them to demonstrate their skill with the bow by shooting from the monastery roof. Both did so, and the arrows fell either side of a lane at Whitby Lathes – more than a mile away. The abbot had two stone pillars erected on the spots where the arrows fell. The pillars survived until the end of the 18th century. The fields on either side were also named after the event: Robin Hood's Close and Little John's Close.

Little John, who was Robin's second-in-command, got his nickname because of his height. He was said to have died at Hathersage, in Derbyshire, and his grave there was reopened in 1784. In it were found the bones of an exceptionally tall man.

J. Gilbert.

ROBIN HOOD & GUY, OF GISBORNE.

Best of both worlds

Police in Venezuela issued a warrant for the arrest of a known criminal. Unfortunately for them, the man's house was built slap across the Venezuela-Colombia border. When they called to arrest him, he ran into his bedroom, locked the door and phoned his lawyer. The bedroom was in Colombian territory and the offence with which he was to be charged was not punishable in that country. The Venezuelan police gave up.

Robin and his men certainly got around. Robin Hood's Bay, away on the Yorkshire coast, was named after him. It was here that the outlaws were reputed to own several boats, which they kept for fishing and for possible escape from the authorities.

On one of his journeys, Robin Hood visited St Mary's Church, Nottingham, where a monk in the congregation recognized him and alerted the sheriff. Robin drew his sword and slew 12 soldiers before being captured. But before he could be brought to trial, Little John led a band of the outlaws into Nottingham and rescued him. They also sought out the monk and murdered him.

But it was Robin Hood's supposed championing of the underdog that made him into a folk hero. His robbing of the rich and gifts to the poor, and his flouting of unpopular authority, became an inspiration to the oppressed peasantry of old England.

On one famous occasion Robin Hood was supposed to have met King Edward II. The story goes that the king, hearing that the herds of royal deer in Sherwood were diminishing because of the appetites of Robin Hood and his band, determined to get rid of the outlaws. So he and his knights disguised themselves as monks and rode into the forest.

They were met by Robin Hood and some of his band, who demanded money. The king gave them £40, saying that was all he had. Robin took £20 for his men and gave the rest back to the king. Edward then produced the royal seal and told the outlaw leader that the king wished to see him in Nottingham. Robin summoned all his men to kneel before the seal and swear their love for the king. They then invited the 'monks' to eat with them – and fed them on the king's venison. Later Edward revealed his identity and pardoned all the outlaws – on condition that they would come to his court and serve him.

The story is told in *A Lytell Geste of Robyn Hood*, published in 1459. It may not be complete fiction – the king was certainly in Nottingham in November 1323 and the story of his action fits what is known of his character.

A few months later, in 1324, the name of Robin Hood appears in the household accounts of Edward II. There is a record of wages paid to him until

November of the same year. After that date, he vanishes into folklore again. Perhaps after enjoying the free life of an outlaw, he was unable to settle in service, even for his king.

Robin Hood's adventures in the forests continued until about 1346 when he is reputed to have died at Kirklees Priory. The prioress there, said to be his cousin Elizabeth de Stainton, is reputed to have hastened his death, when he begged her to help relieve his pain during an illness, by bleeding him until he was too weak to recover.

On his death-bed, so the story concludes, Robin Hood managed to blow his famous hunting horn, which summoned his faithful companion Little John to his side. Robin then shot an arrow from the window of his room and asked to be buried wherever it might fall.

Richard Grafton, who wrote a story about the outlaw band in 1569, said that a tomb was set up at that point by the prioress. But the reason is not flattering to the Robin Hood of popular legend. Grafton wrote:

'The prioresse of the same place caused him to be buried by the highway side, where he had used to rob and spoyle those that passed that way. And upon his grave the sayde prioresse did lay a very fayre stone wherein his name was graven. And the cause why she buried him there was that for the common strangers and travailers, knowyng and seeyng him there buryed, might more safely and without feare take their journeys that way, which they durst not do in the life of the sayd outlawes. And at either end of the sayde tombe was erected a crosse of stone, which is to be seen there at present.'

The stone is no longer there. But the spot claimed to be the grave of Robin Hood can still be seen to this day.

Skulduggery on the high seas

Between 1550 and 1750, thousands of British sailors turned to piracy in the West Indies, the Mediterranean and along the coast of Africa. Some merchants who dabbled in piracy were well rewarded for their services to their country – for most of the victims, mainly French, Portuguese and Spanish, were Britain's enemies.

Francis Drake was knighted for his voyages of discovery, even though Queen Elizabeth I knew he had engaged in piracy, an offence punishable by death; but her 'daring little pirate' had made his queen rich and was an honoured subject.

For other sailors, piracy was a chance to escape a harsh, unrewarding home life and resort to a career of cunning and violence.

John Avery went to sea as the mate of a trading vessel and soon proved his daring by leading a mutiny in 1694. He and his adventurous crew plundered merchant ships. But he established his reputation as the con-man of the high seas by his skill in deceiving victims to part with their valuables without even resorting to violence.

Off the coast of Guinea he took down the skull and crossbones flag, the 'Jolly Roger' trademark of piracy, and hoisted the English flag in its place. The natives, knowing they could trust the English, rowed out and came aboard Avery's ship to trade their valuable gold. It soon became obvious that they had fallen into a clever trap and Avery sent them packing – making sure they left the gold behind.

Avery even tricked fellow pirates into handing over their booty without drawing his cutlass. The pirate captains, based in Madagascar off the African coast, were continually bickering about the way treasure was shared out. Using his great powers of persuasion, Avery convinced the captains that they should entrust their booty to him for safe keeping. Avery kept it so safe that they never saw it – or him – again! But Avery failed to hang on to his ill-gotten gains. A group of scheming merchants tricked him out of his loot and the pirate captain died in poverty in his native county of Devon.

Avery's cheek was surpassed by that of Captain Charles Vane, one of the most impudent pirates of all. In 1718, Britain, under pressure from European countries, sent warships to the Bahamas to put an end to the operations of pirates.

But Vane knew the ships were on their way. When the heavily armed fleet sailed into the pirate bay they were greeted by Vane's vessel sailing straight towards them, flying flags of welcome. The smartly dressed captain and his crew politely saluted the incoming ships and sailed cheekily past them out into the ocean. The salute was returned by the British ships and officers who docked to find they had been duped by the pirate ringleader.

It was a love affair between one of Vane's former seamates, John 'Calico Jack' Rackham, and Anne Bonny that led to one of the most notorious eras in pirate history.

Anne, an adventurous and spirited girl, dressed as a sailor to join Rackham's wild crew so as to be near her beloved Jack. Anne knew she would be in danger if the men found her out, because a woman on board a pirate ship was supposed to be a sign of bad luck. Anne fooled the crew long enough to prove she was as tough as any man on board, and the pirates accepted her. Her trickery had paid off. She revelled in adventure and was always one of the first to leap aboard any Spanish or Portuguese ships under attack.

Sir Francis Drake

When Captain Rackham captured a pirate ship in 1720, Anne found a worthy companion on board – Mary Read, a tough girl who had fled the slums of London for a thrilling and adventurous life.

Both girls got a chance to show their bravery when their ship was attacked by an armed vessel sent from Jamaica to arrest Rackham's pirates. As the faint-hearted men cowered below the decks, Anne and Mary stayed above to fight. When the ship was eventually captured and the crew brought to trial, Anne and Mary both escaped the gallows.

They kept up their trickery to the very end and fooled the judge into letting them go. He believed their story that they were both expecting babies and should be spared!

Romantic reign of the swashbuckling heroes

For 100 years, until the mid-18th century, the entire southern coastline of England was ruled by romantic, swashbuckling bands of smugglers. From the Essex marshes to the rocky cliffs of Land's End they were heroes – 'our brave lads' – to most of the population.

The profits from smuggling were immediate and enormous. From the time of the Norman Conquest, English fleeces were exchanged for fine French wines without more than lip service being paid to the laws that imposed import duties on all foreign luxuries. But not until the 18th century did 'free trade' develop to the point that it involved just about every owner of a lugger that could navigate the Channel on a dark night.

For many a farmer's boy or country inn-keeper's son, a gloomy night and the noises that came through it held few terrors. In fact, by the time he was 16 he might have been starting an apprenticeship that could eventually lead to riches and power.

There were many steps to climb in the 'organization'. He might start by merely holding the horses at one of the interchange points, where London buyers took over smuggled goods for delivery to inland customers. He would almost certainly graduate to the status of tubman, hauling heavy bales and kegs up the beaches to hiding places in caves or lonely churchyards.

He might go on to become a batman – a cudgel-wielding 'heavy' who watched the backs of the tubmen and was ready to spring into action at the first sign of trouble from the Revenue men. Or if the boy's father owned a fishing boat he might begin by actually helping to ferry contraband across the

Channel, learning the route between two coves with no help from the stars.

A lad who knew how to read and write would always be in demand, for the smugglers needed scrupulously kept accounts. In this violent world it could mean sudden death to short-change buyers or sellers. But practically every country craft could be adapted: coopers were needed to fashion cunning barrels with a false skin to hold tea or spirits, and boatbuilders to construct craft with false bottoms and sides or secret compartments where barrels could be hidden.

As the trade developed into a full-scale industry, big money was needed, and in the first half of the 18th century crime syndicates virtually took over the south coast. And, like syndicates in every age, they did not stop at one crime but added extortion, bribery, highway robbery and murder.

It became increasingly obvious to the government that it was losing vast sums of money in duty, and a corps of preventive officers was built up, who, despite the inefficiency and cupidity of senior Customs officials (many of whom were themselves customers of the smuggling rings) and the bribes offered by the smugglers, displayed integrity and courage and faced every sort of danger'to make arrests. Many undoubtedly died in lonely coves or alleyways.

In the year 1733, Revenue men seized 54,000 pounds of tea and 123,000 gallons of brandy – the tip of the iceberg, for they rarely captured more than 10 per cent of an illegal cargo. Tea bought at $3\frac{1}{2}$p a pound in Holland sold in England at anything from 17p to 25p; French brandy bought for £1 a keg fetched £4 in the UK.

This was how Thomas Johnson, who made a fortune out of smuggling and lost £11,000 at the gaming tables, managed to return to his old trade and make a second fortune. And it was in this way that Arthur Gray, who with his brother William masterminded the notorious Hawkhurst Gang, was able to retire (though still planning and financing local operations) to a £10,000 mansion.

At the height of its power, the Hawkhurst Gang, holding sway in Kent and Sussex, was capable of assembling an armed band of 300 men to recover a cargo of tea impounded by the Customs. In October 1747, the men marched from mid-Kent to Dorset, stormed the Poole Customs house and marched back with their booty.

On the outward journey they were cheered through the villages, but as news spread of the sadism with which they had murdered two harmless old men suspected of being informers, the ordinary people started to turn against them. It was the beginning of the end for the gang which, though powerful, relied heavily on the goodwill of the countryside.

Once the gang's influence was broken, and its leaders hanged or transported, its place was taken by the ruthless Ruxley gang, working out of a Hastings cove known as Bo-Peep – (the name, today, of a railway junction). It took 200

A popular print of smugglers from the 1840s

dragoons to subdue the Ruxleys, and even then they might have won the day had they not also been involved in territorial struggles with a gang from Folkestone.

In Devon and Cornwall, contraband regularly travelled the routes followed today by the Plymouth, Roscoff and St Malo ferries. Typical of famous Cornish smugglers was John Corlyon, of Coverack, who, when his boatbuilding business failed, set up as a smuggler and made a handsome living.

There was a strict law against signalling from the shore to a smuggling vessel, but John got round it very simply. If the coast was clear, his wife hung a red shirt from her washing line. If no red shirt appeared, the Revenue men were around. How could they prosecute someone for *not* giving a signal?

Another notable Cornish smuggler was Henry Cuttance, who was captured by a press-gang and taken to sea. He escaped by throwing his hat over the side with a cry of 'man overboard!' As the crew sought the drowning man, Henry slipped over the other side of the vessel and swam the $2\frac{1}{2}$ miles to safety. . . .

Most smugglers encouraged the tall tales that were told about their exploits – and if they had a supernatural twist which kept the credulous away, so much the better. Even today there's a tale of the 'demon drummer of Hurstmonceux Churchyard'; it's a fairly safe bet that the original drummer was a smuggler, detailed to deter the local inhabitants.

Many smuggling yarns became entangled with more ancient folklore. Certainly this was the case with Cruel Coppinger, who so terrorized the people of Welcombe Mouth, on the north Devon and Cornish border, that his name was used to quieten children and became inextricably linked with Viking raiders.

Even today, people of the Romney Marshes, Kent, retell stories about the sinister parson-cum-smuggler named Dr Syn, convinced that they are recounting local history. In fact, the character made his debut in novels written in the 1920s.

Smugglers loved such names, none more so than the Cornish Carters, a father and eight sons who styled themselves the Kings of Prussia because they moored their boats in Prussia Cove.

Jack Rattenbury, who began his smuggling career at the age of nine, working on his uncle's boat, liked to be described as the Rob Roy of the West. Flogged so severely with a rope's end for losing the rudder that he never spoke to his uncle again, Jack, who published his autobiography *Memoirs of a Smuggler* in 1937, was probably the last of the old-style swashbuckling smugglers.

By the early 1800s, times were getting hard for real-life smugglers. By then they had to evade not only an increasingly efficient Customs service but also Navy press-gangs, who recognized them as ideal recruits for their boat-handling and gunnery skills. And desperate men, prepared to accept the gallows or transportation as one of the risks of their profession, often reformed rather than face the harsh discipline of life aboard a warship of Nelson's day.

Chapter Five

Signs of the Times

'For man's greatest crime is to have been born'
Pedro Calderon de la Barca

Computer crooks

The most sophisticated swindlers of modern times are the skilled thieves who are cashing in on the world's fastest-growing crime wave: computer frauds.

Computers, of course, are triumphs of human invention. But these technological marvels can also be extremely stupid – because they never, never ask questions. And even when a computer fraud is uncovered, the company is often too embarrassed to report it to the police.

Probably only about ten per cent of such crimes ever result in police investigation, representing the mere tip of an iceberg whose likely size is illustrated by the fact that in Britain alone more than 50 Scotland Yard detectives are working full-time on £100 million worth of computer frauds.

Two young British computer experts gave up their jobs to form a company advising firms on the dangers of computer-assisted crime. They claimed: 'A computer fraud can be perpetrated in a fraction of a second – the time it takes to blink.' They came across the chief of one computer centre who netted £25,000, from one company, then moved on to take £75,000 from another.

But not every computer cheat is so ambitious. One programmer working for a cigarette company rigged the computer so that it credited him with free savings coupons which he then exchanged for gifts.

Such a fiddle would be no more than child's play to American computer crooks, who currently operate a £100,000 million-a-year growth industry.

One ingenious American bank employee with access to a computer programme devised a system whereby he added 10 cents to every customer service charge of less than $10 and $1 on those above $10. He credited the difference to an account he had opened for himself under the unlikely name of Zzwicke.

The fraud should have gone totally undetected. But the bank; as a promotional stunt, decided to make gifts to the first and last names on their alphabetical list of clients. Last, of course, was Mr Zzwicke!

A variation on the same stunt was played at another bank where an employee ordered the computer to 'lose' 10 cents from every client's account and add it to the last account on the tapes. He then opened an account under a fictitious name beginning with 'Z'.

The fake Mr Z got away with a windfall month after month – until a genuine Mr Z became a client of the bank. His name appeared even further down the alphabet, so when he noticed the inexplicable increase in his monthly account he rang the bank to ask why!

Other fiddles attempted by staff with technical know-how include the case of the man who instructed the computer to ignore all cheques drawn on his own account, and the Washington tax clerk who programmed an Internal Revenue Service computer to list all unclaimed refunds, then sent them to his relatives!

One slippery customer cashed in on a bank computer to the tune of $100,000. He opened an account at a Washington DC branch, thus obtaining a supply of deposit slips. He knew that the computer recognized not the signature on the slips but the individualized magnetic ink symbols printed on them.

So one day he surreptitiously substituted slips from his own paying-in book for those left out on the counters for the convenience of customers who had forgotten their own deposit books. All money paid in on these forms, no matter what names and numbers were entered, went straight into the fiddler's account. After three days he withdrew his balance and vanished.

One of the first Americans to exploit the vulnerability of computers – and company bosses who use them without understanding their intricacies – was accountant Eldon Royce, who stole more than a million dollars between 1963 and 1969.

Angry that his employers – a fruit and vegetables wholesale organization – had failed to keep their promise of profit-sharing, Royce decided to take profits of his own kind.

His firm bought hundreds of different types of produce from hundreds of growers, and sold them to scores of dealers. Thousands of lorry, storage, packing and service transactions were involved. And with prices fluctuating throughout the day, only a computer could keep track.

Royce planned his rake-off carefully. He added fractions of a cent to the price of items bought by his company, and took fractions of a cent off the cost of items it sold. The computer then spread the differences across the various accounts, so that the books balanced. Every so often, Royce drained off his secret surplus by writing a cheque to one of the 17 bogus companies he had set up.

Eventually Royce fell victim to his own cleverness. Exhausted by the constant need for vigilance and meticulous accounting, he realized, when his firm's profits suddenly shot up, he could not put a stop to the rake-offs without

---

The boomerang brick

A young, would-be burglar stopped outside a jeweller's shop in the English seaside resort of Brighton one wintry night in 1981. From beneath his coat he produced a brick. He took aim and threw it at the window. The brick hit the reinforced glass, rebounded and knocked the raider unconscious.

Stanley Rifkin speaks to reporters upon his release from jail on bail

arousing suspicions. He confessed and was jailed for 10 years.

But the master of computer frauds was the man who became a multi-millionaire in minutes.

Stanley Rifkin had once worked as a computer programmer at a Los Angeles bank. Since the staff still knew him, he had no trouble in gaining access to the bank's wire room, where he memorized the day's codes. He then plugged in to the computer terminal and transferred $10 million to his own account!

Rifkin was caught only after a woman accomplice confided in a man she believed was a crooked bank employee. Unfortunately, he turned out to be an FBI agent.

Even FBI agents were surprised when they caught the person who had tuned into a computer to erase 10 million items from its memory bank. The culprit was just 13 years of age!

Using a phone in his New York school, the boy had called up a computer-communications network's ex-directory number. He then kept the direct line to the computer constantly engaged while he tried various codes to gain access to the system. Eventually, by trial and error, he managed it.

The 13-year-old later explained that his ruse began as a game when classmates suggested that they try to order the computer from the local Coca-Cola distributor to deliver free Coke to all their homes!

The clerk who 'invested' his bank's £32 million

Marc Colombo was a little man with big ideas. As a lowly foreign-exchange dealer working for a British bank in Switzerland, he saw fortunes changing hands daily. Fluctuations in the values of the world's leading currencies opened up enticing opportunities for men shrewd and brave enough to buy when the price was right and sell at a profit.

Colombo, a handsome 28-year-old, was one of only 16 employees at the Lugano branch of Lloyds Bank International. Lugano was the smallest of the organization's 170 branches – yet after Marco Colombo had finished with it, its name was better known than any other in the world!

The Middle East war of 1973 led to an oil embargo by Arab states. This sent foreign exchange rates crazy and made Colombo believe that the dollar's value would tumble while the Swiss franc remained strong. So he struck what is

Marc Colombo, foreign exchange dealer and Egidio Moembelli, branch manager

known as a forward deal with other international money dealers.

In November 1973, he agreed that – at current rates – his bank would buy US $34 million with Swiss francs the following January. He thought that the dollar's value would have fallen by that time and he would be able to use cheap dollars to buy back his francs. But instead the dollar went from strength to strength.

He now realized he had cost Lloyds about £1 million. He wasn't too worried. After all, his bank had just declared half-yearly profits of £78 million.

One person who had to be kept in the dark, however, was the bank manager, Egidio Mombelli. Having worked for Mombelli for a year, Colombo knew that, if he kept up a show of confidence, his boss would not suspect a thing. But he had to recoup his losses.

Without Lloyd's knowledge, Colombo continued to speculate. After pinning his faith on the dollar falling, which it did not, he changed his tactics, believing it would go on rising. Instead it eventually fell.

Lloyds had a £700,000 daily limit on debts or holdings. Colombo went way above this. The only records he kept were in his diary. The bank and the Swiss

banking authorities had no clue as to what was going on.

And neither did his colleagues or the unfortunate Mombelli. To them, Colombo was a hard-working, trustworthy employee.

But everything changed in August, 1974. It was then that a Lloyds Bank man in London was told by a top French banker that their Lugano branch had 'reached its limit with us'. Lloyds' offices in Queen Victoria Street were on the alert. Phone calls showed that a German bank had also been doing huge currency deals with Lugano.

A plane from London took Lloyds chiefs to Lugano the next day. They interviewed Colombo, Mombelli and the man in charge of all three of Lloyds' Swiss branches, Karl Senft. A mass of documents and the three Swiss employees accompanied the bankers back to London.

It took a full weekend to sort out the mess. At the end, Lloyds men were shocked to find that there was £235 million still tied up in the dangerous 'forward' deals. Colombo had believed in putting all his golden eggs in one basket. A sum greater than the combined capital and reserves of all three Lloyds banks in Switzerland was staked. The bank records had shown a mere £36,000.

Lloyds had to call in the Bank of England to unscramble things. The Governor himself agreed to allow them to transfer vast quantities of money to Lugano so that the deals set up by Colombo would be honoured.

The bank's international money market director, Robert Gras, also had his work cut out. He had to buy in the dollars Colombo had agreed to sell, without people realizing. It was a tricky operation which could be made vastly more expensive if international money men knew Lloyds were over a barrel.

It took three weeks of quietly feverish activity to settle the debts and, at the end, the world was told that Lloyds in Switzerland had lost a horrific £32 million. Never before – in Switzerland or in Britain – had such a loss been known. Lloyds' London shares immediately lost £20 million when chairman Sir Eric Faulkner broke the news.

By that time, Colombo and Mombelli and their families had gone into hiding away from the eager questioning of the Press.

A year later both appeared in Lugano's court on charges of criminal mismanagement, falsification of documents and violations of the Swiss banking code. Colombo denied that he had accepted illegal commissions or had any criminal intent, but he did admit breaking the dealing limits and conducting unauthorized transactions. He also slammed Lloyds Lugano branch for its lax systems of checking and criticized the 'frustrating' spending limits that had been placed on him. Colombo seemed unmoved when the prosecution described him as the 'mouse that made Lloyds tremble' and accused him of throwing money about like a man at a casino.

'Being a foreign-exchange dealer is always a hazardous operation,' he told them. 'It is a gambler's profession.'

He was unrepentant about the extent of his speculation. 'There was the pride of the foreign-exchange dealer who will not admit failure,' he told the court. 'I was at all times convinced that I could recoup my losses, but it only takes something a little unforeseen to upset the market. I was a prisoner of events.'

Even if Colombo had ended up with a profit he would still have faced the sack for breaking banking rules. But he claimed he would have netted £11 million for Lloyds if they had allowed his currency deals to stand.

Mombelli, 41, admitted that he had never understood what was happening and said he had signed papers without realizing what they were.

'It's a foreign-exchange Mafia,' Mombelli said after the trial. 'For every dealer you need at least four administrators to check what he is doing. They do things no ordinary banker understands.'

The two men walked from the court, much to Lloyds' amazement. Colombo received an 18-month suspended sentence and Mombelli one of six months, with a £300 fine each. The judge accepted that the two had not been out to line their own pockets.

Would you credit it!

Everybody has one birth certificate. But in America in the late 1970s, too many people had more than one – and officials estimated that it was costing the country a staggering £20 billion a year.

The cashless society had gone credit-card crazy. And as criminals had fewer chances to grab huge hauls of money, a new breed of con-man sprang up, ready to cash in on false credentials.

It was all based on the birth certificate. For a small fee, and the answers to a few questions, anyone could obtain a copy of his or her certificate – or anybody else's. Every year more than 10 million certificates were requested, and 80 per cent of these were despatched by post. Checks on applications were minimal.

Armed with the precious birth certificate, criminals could create a total 'paper person'. They could claim social security cards or driving licences, open bank accounts, collect welfare benefits, obtain credit cards.

In greatest demand were certificates of people who had died in infancy. There was then no danger of meeting the person whose identity had been usurped. And once a safe new identity had been established, all things were possible. . . .

In Chicago the authorities arrested a welfare scrounger – and discovered that as well as milking the Illinois coffers of £80,000, she had used 250 aliases in 16 different states to obtain social security benefits.

She had posed as an unemployed mother or as a widow. She used the names of eight different dead 'husbands' and at least 31 addresses. She had claimed for 24 children. When she came to court, even her own lawyer was not sure he knew her right name.

In California, well-dressed con-men called at the homes of people advertising expensive cars for sale in local newspapers. Introducing themselves with false identity cards, they agreed a price, produced a banker's draft, and drove off – taking care to leave after the banks had shut for the day.

Next morning, when the car seller discovered that the cheque was worthless, the gang had already disposed of the car. Using fraudulently obtained documents, they had sold it to a legitimate dealer – and disappeared.

In Los Angeles, the murder-suicide of lovers Patty Bledsoe and Robert Hinkley in 1974 revealed a more sinister confidence trick. The couple had credit cards, driving licences and social security cards in at least four names other than their own. They had used them as proof of identity in cashing counterfeit pay cheques from the Western Gillette Trucking Company. In one weekend, they collected £9,000.

By the time the banks were refusing to honour the worthless cheques, the couple were involved in the second stage of their plot – using the money to buy cocaine in Colombia, then re-entering America on forged passports to sell it on the streets.

Apart from criminals, illegal immigrants were believed to be using the birth certificate trick to establish legitimate bona fides. And in 1976 there were estimated to be eight million of them in the U.S., an annual tax burden of nearly £7,000 million.

A series of 'paper people' scandals forced the Government to act. An 80-strong Federal Advisory Committee on False Identification was set up to investigate. And after a year's deliberations, it recommended matching birth and death records, and criminal penalties for fraudulent use of birth certificates. Stricter standards were also introduced to vet applicants for driving licences and welfare benefits.

The day the bubble burst

It was the greatest financial catastrophe in Britain's history: the day when the so-called South Sea Bubble burst. The Bubble was a massive fraud perpetrated by the South Sea Company, which was formed in 1710 and which collapsed spectacularly exactly 10 years later.

The aims of the company had been honest but its aspirations grandiose. The South Sea Company quite simply invited the public to invest in it on such a scale that the profits would be sufficient to pay off the entire national debt.

Britain's growing middle class rushed to put their money into the venture. So successful was it that hundreds of other get-rich-quick companies sprang up in its wake. An infectious gambling fever swept the country.

One of the new investment companies floated shares for building pirate-proof ships, another went in for planting mulberry trees and breeding silkworms, and a third started importing jackasses to improve the quality of British mules.

There was even a company formed for insuring girls against losing their virginity!

Yet some of the businesses were quite soundly based. One revolutionary venture was 'for paying pensions to widows' and another 'for insuring people against thefts and robberies'.

The boom lasted until 1720, by which time the South Sea Company had amassed enormous debts through inexpert trade deals. But the momentum behind the company was too great to allow it to admit defeat – and bankruptcy.

Sentence a walkover

Two students convicted of siphoning about three gallons of petrol from a parked car got four miles to the gallon. The court at Monroe, North Carolina, sentenced them to walk 12 miles.

So a new share issue was put on the market to pay for the company's past mistakes. They were all snapped up.

Then the rumours began. The panic to sell was unprecedented. Nothing like it was again seen until the Wall Street crash 200 years later. As the shares fell and panic swept the land, the law stepped in, barring all companies trading without a licence. The result was commercial chaos. Hundreds of firms went bankrupt and hundreds of investors committed suicide.

It was at this point that the Prime Minister, Sir Robert Walpole, intervened. He realized that the South Sea Company must be rescued. He ordered the Bank of England to take over £9 million of the South Sea stock and the wealthy East India Company to be responsible for a similar amount.

He also ordered an examination of the South Sea's books. The result: £2 million was confiscated from the estates of dishonest directors and distributed among the badly battered shareholders.

Also well satisfied were those in the know who got out before the Bubble burst. Among them was Spencer Compton, Speaker of the House of Commons, who reputedly made a £80,000 profit.

Cops who stung them in style

In the hit movie, *The Sting*, Robert Redford and Paul Newman played a couple of con-men who cheated a gang boss out of a fortune in a gambling den. It was all fun and fiction – but it did hold a lesson for America's hard-pressed police forces. It showed them how to play the crooks and con-men at their own game.

In 1976, shortly after the film's release, federal agents tried out a sting operation in California, setting up a string of seven fake warehouses for receiving stolen goods. The Sting Squad, posing as crooks, brought up every crime haul offered, from jewellery to guns and stolen cars. Contraband and stolen property worth millions of dollars was recovered and more than 200 arrests were made in the Los Angeles area.

Most of the crooks were rounded up by inviting them to parties in celebration of their profitable crimes. Among the men booked was a professional killer who offered the con-men cops his services to get rid of underworld rivals.

Since then, Sting Squads have pulled off more than 50 successful similar operations, recovering over $250 million in stolen goods and putting more than 200 crime bosses behind bars.

But the greatest sting of all was pulled in Flint, Michigan, where the local Mr Big was a 'fence' – a receiver of stolen goods – known to his many underworld associates as Lucky. About $1 million of hot property had passed through his hands up to the time of the announcement of his untimely death.

Sixty crooks turned up for the funeral service. But no sooner had they taken their seats than the doors burst open and every man in the room was arrested – by the Sting Squad!

The whole fencing operation had been masterminded by undercover federal agents. Mr Big was really Walter Ryerson, a 40-year-old Treasury Department investigator. He grew a beard, let his hair grow, wore expensive suits and spent months infiltrating the local crime ring. And he was in on the kill with the rest of the squad at the funeral service held in his honour.

A further 300 crooks were rounded up. Ryerson had video-taped and recorded all his business transactions. As one crook said: 'You just don't know who you can trust these days.'

Million-dollar bank roll

Most folk would, without hesitation, hand in any lost valuables found in the street. But the public's honesty was sorely tested the day that someone mislaid a million dollars in the centre of an American city in 1981.

The money belonged to a Philadelphia bank and was being taken by a security firm to its headquarters less than three miles away. The money was stacked on a metal trolley in the back of a security van.

Half-way along the route, it would seem that a series of bumps 'tricked' the automatic mechanism on the locks into opening the van doors. The trolley, with its million-dollar load, rolled out of the van and trundled down the street.

The guards sitting up front in the security van did not know anything was amiss and drove into the distance. Witnesses said that the trolley ran along the street until it bumped into a pavement. A passing car drew to a halt, two men stepped out, gleefully loaded the two canvas bags of cash and drove off.

Police later interrogated the guards, suspecting a plot. But a detective said: 'These guys are as pure as snow. We are satisfied there was no conspiracy. It was just an incredible accident.'

All the missing money was in old banknotes and the security firm held out little hope of tracing it. They said they 'still hoped these people will turn out to be honest passers-by and will return the money' – and they offered a $50,000 reward to the two fortune finders.

There were no takers. . . .

Lousy luck that landed a couple in jail

Every con-trick or deception needs a certain amount of help from lady luck. But in 1938, even the man behind the crime could not believe his good fortune when an incredible string of coincidences conspired to place the wrong man in jail – and put him within an ace of getting away with £18,000.

Just before Christmas, banknotes worth the equivalent of £9,000 disappeared over a weekend from the safe of a small business in the Hungarian capital of Budapest. Police questioned the owner and his £100-a-month book-keeper cashier, the only men who knew the combination. The cashier had been the last to leave the office on the Friday before the crime, and his fingerprints were the only ones on the safe.

The case took a dramatic turn three weeks later. Detectives learned that on the Monday following the robbery, a woman had opened an £8,500 bank

---

Raiders on the run!

Thieves were on the run after raiding a pharmacy in the southern English village of Alresford, Hampshire . . . their £100 haul of tablets included 600 laxatives. Police, who warned that the tablets would produce a 'violent reaction', said: 'We've no idea how long these men will remain loose.'

> ### Living for licks
> A 14-year-old London boy, accused with his brother of stealing £50, told police that he spent £25 of the money in two weeks – on ice-cream.

account using the name Anna Nagy. It was a common name in Hungary – but police knew it was also the maiden name of the cashier's wife, who was eight months pregnant.

Inquiries revealed that the couple had spent the equivalent of £700 on a Christmas shopping spree. Their purchases included a radiogram, a baby carriage, and furniture for a nursery. Circumstantial evidence seemed to implicate the cashier. He was arrested and thrown into jail while police prepared the prosecution.

In those days, bank depositors in Hungary were not required to give an address. So the only hope of identifying Anna Nagy rested with the teller who took her money, and her signature on the deposit slip. Here again, a twist of fate stacked the odds against the cashier. The bank teller had died of a heart attack before police could interview him. And though there was no similarity between the autograph of the woman who deposited the money and the cashier's wife, police argued convincingly that she would want to disguise her handwriting, and be under strong emotional pressure, thus accounting for the shaky, uncertain writing.

When the case came to court, the prosecution said every Anna Nagy on the register of voters had been checked. And despite extensive publicity in the newspapers, no unregistered woman of that name had come forward. The evidence was considered conclusive. The cashier was convicted and jailed.

There the matter might have rested, had it not been for the handwriting expert called in by the Budapest criminal court to compare the two signatures.

The graphologist, Hanna Sulner, remained convinced that the woman who had opened the bank account was much older than the cashier's wife, possibly with a physical infirmity that made writing difficult. She went to see the cashier in his cell. He was bewildered and defeated, protesting his innocence with resigned despair. Their Christmas spree was with money saved over their four years of marriage, he explained. He had opened the safe on the Friday, but only to take out wages.

Next Hanna visited the wife in hospital. She had given birth to her baby, but was suffering from a nervous breakdown after the ordeal of the court case. Hanna was convinced she had not deposited the cash, but the distressed woman only sobbed: 'They'll never believe you.'

The couple's lawyer was equally gloomy. Why, despite nationwide publicity, had nobody come forward to claim the cash?

Then, at last, there came a stroke of luck. Hanna was discussing the case with a doctor friend over lunch, and reacted angrily to suggestions that she was letting her sympathy run away with her judgement.

'It's a question of science,' she snapped. 'That deposit slip was signed by someone much older than the cashier's wife, somebody with a handicap that made writing difficult.'

'You mean she could have been ill?' asked the doctor.

'Yes.'

'Have the hospitals been checked?'

It was so devastatingly simple that Hanna cursed herself for not thinking of it before.

The first hospital she tried had an Anna Nagy, who had already been questioned before being admitted to give birth to twins. The second knew of no Anna Nagy. But the third. . . .

Here was the answer to the mystery. A middle-aged woman from a village near the Rumanian border had been admitted just before Christmas for a serious eye operation. She had travelled to Budapest bringing her savings, and had put them in the bank for safe-keeping. Now she was convalescing, half-blind and unable to read newspapers.

Hanna asked her to sign her name on a slip of paper. The signature was identical to that on the bank form. The cashier was completely exonerated on appeal, and released to build a new life with his wife and child.

His place in prison was taken by the real culprit. He had crept into the deserted office over the weekend and raided the safe, wearing gloves. He knew the business would be reimbursed by the insurance company, which would double his takings from the crime. For he was the owner of the firm.

Grave justice

A gravestone in a churchyard in Sheldon, Vermont, bears this epitaph to an unknown burglar shot while robbing a store on October 13, 1905: 'Here lies a burglar – this stone was bought with money found on him.'

Chapter Six

The Spoils of War

'War is much too serious a thing to be left
to military men'
Briand

The love cheats who listened in at Madame Kitty's

Madame Kitty's pleasure palace was the talk of Berlin's high society. All a newcomer had to do was turn up at her door and use the codeword: 'I come from Rothenburg'.

She would produce a lavish photograph album of her 20 most ravishing beauties, complete with personal details . . . and the client would take his pick. After a 10-minute wait, savouring the delights to come over a generous drink, he would be confronted by the girl who whisked him off to her boudoir and pandered to his every whim.

So enticing were Madame Kitty's ladies that visiting dignitaries, army generals and embassy staff could not resist sampling the pleasures behind the elegant third-floor doors of the fashionable house.

But sex was seldom what it seemed at 11 Giesebrechtstrasse. And the most satisfied smiles were usually on the faces of men who never availed themselves of the establishment's facilities.

The house that attracted the elite of Germany's diplomatic corps and armed forces had, in fact, been set up by a hard-headed Nazi intelligence chief who was banking on customers abandoning their common sense amid their sensual delights.

He was not disappointed. For months, indiscreet pillow talk gave eavesdropping Gestapo officers the evidence they needed to keep Hitler one step ahead ir controlling his own people, and manipulating leaders of other countries.

But the great deception eventually came unstuck . . . because another con-man got in on the act.

Operation Kitty had been sparked off in 1939 by Gruppenführer Reinhard Heydrich, later notorious as the Butcher of Prague, but then the feared, ruthless, ambitious head of the Nazi SS network.

For some time he had been worried by careless security leaks in high places. With war fast approaching, it was essential to identify and eliminate loose tongues. The quickest way of doing that was to put suspects through the passion test, tempting them to blabber with wine and beautiful women.

Obersturmführer Walter Schellenberg, cunning chief of the SD – the Nazi central security organization – was ordered to infiltrate an exclusive brothel and enlist girls willing to pass on information they overheard.

But Schellenberg was not a man to do things by halves. The order gave him the idea for an ingenious surveillance blanket check. Instead of using a brothel, he would take it over completely. A team of hand-picked, specially-trained beauties would file reports immediately after sex-and-secrets sessions with celebrities.

And just in case anything slipped their minds, every room would be bugged, so that other agents in a basement control room could record every word, sigh and exclamation of bliss.

Only one bordello fitted the bill perfectly . . . and fate had made taking it over a simple matter.

Kitty Schmidt was then 57. For years her pension had been known as the most luxurious house of ill repute in the city, frequented by the most distinguished and influential figures in German society. Her charges were high, but that was the price clients paid for complete discretion.

Hitler's rise to power had disturbed Kitty. Rough and ready Brownshirts were replacing the gentle Jewish bankers and businessmen on whom she had built her reputation, and the police were no longer so obliging about letting her operate without harassment.

Cautious Kitty began transferring takings to London via Jewish refugees she helped smuggle abroad. By 1939 she had amassed several thousand pounds in British banks – and on June 28 she left Berlin to start spending them. She got as far as the German-Dutch border. SD shadows had tailed her from the capital, and brought her back to Gestapo HQ in Prinz Albrechtstrasse.

Schellenberg was waiting with a bulky dossier and a list of crimes: helping Jews to escape, illegally exchanging German marks, illegally transferring money abroad, attempting to leave Germany without permission, using a forged passport. The charges spelled death or an open-ended term in a concentration camp.

But the Nazi was prepared to be reasonable. 'If you can do something for me,' he said, 'I may be able to do something for you.'

Kitty, with no room to bargain, agreed to his astounding suggestions. She would hand her brothel over to the SD, ask for no explanation, do what she was told, and sign an official secrets document which meant death if she divulged one word of what was going on.

Workmen moved into 11 Giesebrechtstrasse to give it a sinister refurbishment. The interior was gutted and rewired, with microphones in every bedroom, lounge and corridor. A multi-core cable ran along the guttering, down a drainpipe, and into the bricked-off cellar.

Here five monitoring desks, each with two record turntables, were installed. Conversations from ten rooms could be recorded simultaneously on wax discs.

Meanwhile, SD Untersturmführer Karl Schwarz was finding girls to coax the unwary into filling the records with indiscreet words. Berlin's vice squad carried out an unprecedented number of raids on brothels, nightclubs and street corners. Hundreds of girls were grilled, then rejected as 'emotionally unreliable'.

Psychiatrists, doctors, language consultants and university professors all helped Schwarz whittle his short-list of 90 girls down to 20 in seven days of non-stop tests and interrogation.

The breathtaking beauties they selected were taken to a sealed-off wing of the officers' academy at Sonthofen. For seven weeks they went through a gruelling course of foreign languages, unarmed combat, marksmanship, foreign and home politics, economics, use of codes and ciphers.

They had to memorize charts of military uniforms and decorations. German radio interviewers demonstrated how to solicit secrets in seemingly innocent conversation.

By March 1940 all was ready for the launch of Operation Kitty. Schwarz briefed the madame in her newly redecorated parlour. 'Carry on as before', she was told. 'Welcome all your old customers. Keep on your existing girls.'

'But every so often, we will send along someone special. On no account introduce him to one of your regular staff, but show him this album of 20 girls. When he makes his choice, phone for her. She will arrive in 10 minutes. You will not discuss the client with her, and she will leave immediately he has gone.'

When Kitty asked how she would recognize the special visitors, she was told: 'They will use the codeword "I come from Rothenburg."'

Twelve days later, a young SS officer on leave was used to test the system. Schwarz and his colleagues tuned in as the unsuspecting man prattled about his home, his relatives and his devotion to the Führer.

But the girl had learned her lessons well. When she flattered his fighting spirit, he began bragging of his unit's imminent transfer, adding: 'If you ask me, the Führer's got his eye on Sweden.'

Schwarz was delighted with the success of the eavesdropping, even if he did have to arrange a court martial. And there were many more to follow as the supply of Rothenburg romeos was stepped up.

Soon the 20 girls were making love round the clock as special guests outnumbered genuine customers. The Gestapo had to send in extra food and drink as the celebrities exhausted Kitty's ration supplies.

During 1940 nearly 10,000 people climbed to the third floor. And in one month, 3,000 love sessions went on record.

Count Galeazzo Ciano, Italy's Foreign Minister, amazed listening agents one night with a tirade about Hitler's shortcomings as statesman, soldier and lover. When Schwarz forwarded a transcript to the Führer, relations between the two countries were never the same again.

In September, Schellenberg himself took over the earphones when Nazi foreign minister Joachim von Ribbentrop arrived at Kitty's salon with his

Gruppenführer Reinhard Heydrich, later known as the Butcher of Prague

Spanish opposite number, Don Ramon Serrano Suner. He overheard a bizarre Spanish plan to occupy Gibraltar, and was able to warn SS chief Heinrich Himmler in time to squash it.

Another visitor was Major-General Sepp Dietrich, commander of Hitler's personal bodyguard. He dropped no secrets, but caused problems of a different sort – he demanded all 20 girls for a party. Schwarz rounded up as many as he could – and Dietrich amazed the listeners with his stamina.

Only once did the codeword fail . . . when a soldier turned up who really was from the town of Rothenburg.

And the only time the recording and listening equipment was turned off was during Reinhard Heydrich's increasingly frequent 'tours of inspection'.

By this time, though, the Germans were not the only people listening in at Madame Kitty's.

Towards the end of 1940, Lljubo Kolchev, a junior press secretary at the Rumanian Embassy stumbled over some wires as he wandered down Giesebrechtstrasse.

Untersturmführer Schwarz, supervising the rerouting of cables from the No. 11 cellar to a new recording post at SD HQ in Meineckestrasse, automatically reached out to prevent the man falling. Schwarz had no way of knowing that the casual pedestrian was really Roger Wilson, a British spy.

Wilson had heard the 'Rothenberg' stories going round the embassy. Now, as he saw SD men in civilian clothes pretending to be workmen, and the multi-core cable in the drainpipe, he knew those stories were fact.

London ordered him to keep tabs on the salon without rousing suspicion, and Wilson became a regular visitor, keeping his eyes and ears open. Later a communications expert was sent in to fix wire taps to three of the wires in the cable.

From December 1940 until 1943, when Operation Kitty was closed down, Britain and the Allies shared some of its most intimate secrets.

But the salon's heyday had passed. Bombing raids reduced the flood of celebrities to a trickle, and Heydrich was increasingly using the love-and-listen

---

Case for the defence

A man who pleaded not guilty to purse-snatching in Tulsa, Oklahoma, decided to present his own defence. He began by asking the woman victim: 'Did you get a good look at my face when I grabbed your bag?' Not surprisingly, he was found guilty and jailed.

network to settle old scores with rivals in the Nazi hierarchy. Discipline was becoming ever more lax, with the 20 sex spies often staying on at the brothel for strictly forbidden drinks parties.

In July 1942 a bomb finally landed on Kitty's empire, scattering her elegant furniture and rich drapes all over Giesebrechtstrasse. Schwarz threw a ring of soldiers round the street, removed any incriminating evidence of the bugging, then set Kitty up again in the undamaged ground floor of the building.

Within a year, it was all over. The SD handed the house back to Kitty, and most of the beautiful agents decided to stay with her. Kitty had to sign another pledge to reveal nothing of what had gone on. It was a promise she kept until her death in 1954, aged 71.

Walter Schellenberg, the man who dreamed up the great deception, was arrested by the Allies in 1945. But they never got their hands on the 25,000 discs recorded during the operation. They vanished from the files at Gestapo headquarters as the Russians entered the smoking rubble of what had been Hitler's capital.

Do they still exist? No-one can be sure. But they were glimpsed once, in 1963, by author Peter Norden in a top-secret storeroom at the headquarters of the East German state security service in East Berlin.

The captain of Köpenick

Uniforms fascinated 57-year-old Wilhelm Voigt. After all, he had been familiar with them, in one form or another, for quite some time. Indeed, for no less than 27 years he had worn prison uniform himself, serving sentences for various petty crimes. Recently released from jail, he now looked in awe and envy at the smart captain's uniform hanging in the window of a second-hand shop in Potsdam near Berlin.

The price tag on it was equal to a whole week's wages from Voigt's job as a cobbler. But he didn't hesitate for long. He walked into the shop, tried the uniform for size and bought it on the spot.

It was 1906 and life held very little hope for the ex-jailbird. What the poor cobbler yearned for was respect from others, pride in himself and a little nest-egg for his old age. With his newly acquired uniform, he saw the chance of getting the lot.

Voigt first made a careful study of the local militia – how they marched, how they saluted, how they issued and obeyed commands. Then he decided on a dress rehearsal for his grand plan. A brewers' exhibition in Berlin gave him the opportunity.

The exhibition was well under way, the hall crowded, when 'Captain' Wilhelm Voigt stalked through the door. At every stand, there were nods from the tradesmen and shy but admiring sideways glances from the ladies. This flattered the ex-convict immensely, but what really delighted him was the reaction whenever he passed a soldier. The man would immediately leap to attention and salute stiffly. Voigt's dummy run had worked perfectly.

The gleeful cobbler then put the final touches to his master-plan. It was a scheme that took full advantage of the Prussian awe of authority and at the same time paid back the Kaiser's pompous government officials and bureaucrats who had refused to return his passport and identity card following his last stint in jail.

Voigt polished up his buttons and donned his uniform once more. Then he marched off to a big Berlin barracks and waited for his chance. It was not long before a corporal and five grenadiers marched towards the barracks gate.

'Corporal, where are you taking those men?' barked Voigt.

'Back to the barracks, sir,' said the corporal.

'Turn them round and follow me,' Voigt snapped. 'I have an urgent mission for them on direct orders of the Kaiser himself.'

The phoney captain led his little army back up the road. On the way, he ordered four more soldiers to fall in and follow him. With 10 men behind him, Wilhelm was now a force to be reckoned with. So commandeering a bus was easy – in the Kaiser's name, of course.

Their destination was Köpenick, an outlying district of Berlin. Once there, Voigt lined his troops up for inspection, then marched them off to the town hall.

'You're under arrest,' he snarled, bursting into the parlour of Dr Langerhans, the burgomaster.

'Where is your warrant?' asked the startled official.

'I am acting under orders,' replied Voigt. 'And my warrant is the men I command.'

The burgomaster, himself a reserve officer, knew that orders were orders. But he was still concerned that the 'captain' looked rather old for his role, and that his cap badge was upside down! Again he demanded his authority.

This time Voigt's rage knew no bounds. He said he had been sent by Berlin to check on missing municipal funds, that Dr Langerhans was suspected of fraud and that he was being placed under guard immediately. He then summoned the Inspector of Police and told him to get his men onto the streets in case of public disorder.

Despatching some of his men to collect the mayor's wife, Voigt turned his attention to the borough treasurer's office. 'You are under arrest,' he told the official. 'I am ordered to confiscate all your funds.' Fortunately the treasurer did not suspect that anything was wrong.

Meekly, the treasurer unlocked his safe and handed over 4,000 marks, worth about £650. Wilhelm handed over a bogus receipt, signed 'Von Aloesam, Captain, Guards Regiment.'

Ordering his men to hold the prisoners outside, Voigt eagerly ransacked the office, looking for a passport and identity card. But this time he was clearly out of luck.

Unsuccessful in his search for a new identity, Voigt decided to play the captain for a little longer. He ordered the Inspector of Police to commandeer a number of carriages from wealthy townsfolk and had the entire town council bundled inside and sent off to Berlin under armed guard. There they were delivered to General Moltke who, realizing the absurdity of the situation, roared with laughter and sent them packing.

The general also took the precaution of sending an armed party back to Köpenick to arrest the 'captain' before he did any more damage. But they arrived too late. Voigt had fled.

He had scuttled back to the railway station retrieving a bundle of civilian clothes he had previously deposited in the left luggage office. A quick change, and the captain was Wilhelm Voigt again – speeding back to Berlin on the first train.

Next day, the newspapers were full of the exploits of the mystery man who had taken authority down a peg or two. Voigt was delighted, even when a 25,000-mark reward was put on his head. But as the days went by and still no culprit had been arrested, he began to feel cheated of the recognition he had earned. So he planted a photograph to help lead police to him. And, after ten days, they came to arrest him at breakfast time.

The trial was a sensation. The poor little cobbler who had pricked the pomposity of both army and government was a national hero. And there were great rumblings of discontent when the judge handed out a heavy four-year sentence.

But Voigt didn't serve the full term. The Kaiser, who was said to have muttered 'lovable scoundrel' when told of his exploits, gave way to public sympathy and pardoned him after 20 months.

At last Wilhelm Voigt left jail a famous figure, his ambitions fulfilled. All except one – money. The 4,000 marks had been recovered almost intact and Voigt was again penniless. He was forced to perform a vaudeville act in the United States . . . until an invitation from a rich Berlin dowager changed his life. Captivated by the sheer audacity of his deeds, the old lady granted him a life pension which enabled him to retire in comfort to Luxembourg. He died there in 1922 at the age of 72.

Satan in satin

When his Great Army of the Potomac was crushed at Bull Run, Abraham Lincoln knew there had been treason in his government – and that behind the treachery was a beautiful but deadly woman. He called on General George B. McClellan to take command of the shattered Union Army. And together they turned to Allan Pinkerton, founder of Pinkerton's Detective Agency and internationally known manhunter. Now he was to become a hunter of women. Specifically, his prey would be Mrs Rose O'Neal Greenhow – 'Rebel Rose' – whose Washington spy ring was like a noose around the Union throat.

Rich, brilliant and seductive, the 44-year-old widow lived in an elegant mansion that had become the favourite gathering place of Washington's elite. She made no secret of her Southern sympathies or her flaming love affairs. She claimed to have been James Buchanan's mistress and the power behind his presidency. She also boasted that her current affair with Senator Harold Wilson had led to the trapping of Union forces at Manassas and the Bull Run catastrophe. There would later be documentary proof of her claim when Rebel archives were taken after the fall of the Confederate capital of Richmond, Virginia.

As chairman of the Senate's Military Affairs Committee, Wilson knew Lincoln's secret war plans. He had confided those secrets to Rose Greenhow, who routed them to another of her lovers in the Confederate high command, using as courier a female operative who crossed Union lines disguised as a farm-girl.

The contest between Rose and Pinkerton became a classic duel of wits. Rose made the first move, inviting him to a lavish house party where she tried every blandishment on the no-nonsense Scot. But when Pinkerton failed to take the bait, she became his deadliest enemy.

In the weeks that followed, Pinkerton and his men kept a constant watch on her home. Rose knew of the surveillance and openly laughed at it. Her own female operatives, all stunningly beautiful, continued to pass in and out of the house, and the great of Washington still vied for her favours.

The treacherous Wilson was a constant caller, and General McClellan angrily told Pinkerton that military secrets were reaching the enemy daily. Without further delay, Pinkerton arrested Mrs Greenhow in her home. Under the lady's furious eyes, he ordered a search of the premises and turned up damning evidence.

There was the cipher by which she had communicated with the enemy.

Rose O'Neal Greenhow with her daughter in the courtyard of the Old Capitol Prison   147

There were Senator Wilson's passionate love letters. There was a list of Rose's couriers and fellow conspirators, most of them wealthy and powerful. Worse, there were copies of official information on the movement of troops, the sizes and quantities of ordnance, and blueprints of the forts defending the city.

The grim-faced Pinkerton wanted Rose and her co-conspirators hanged, but Lincoln and McClellan vetoed the idea. Some of the traitors were so highly placed that the already shaky administration could have toppled.

For five months Lincoln wrestled with the problem, while Pinkerton kept Rose under house arrest in her home. But on January 18, 1862, she was transferred to Washington's Old Capitol Prison.

No spy in history has enjoyed kinder prison treatment. With the Greenhow fortune still at her disposal, she was given a suite of rooms on the second floor where guards brought her catered meals and champagne from her own cellars.

In Rose's case, prison discipline was suspended entirely. Her powerful friends came and went at will, and the guards retired politely when Senator Wilson was a guest. Another frequent caller was Gustavus V. Fox, Assistant Secretary of the Navy, who was reckless enough to divulge the government's naval plans.

To everyone's surprise, Rose had taken up knitting, and balls of coloured wool were delivered to her through the Provost Marshal's office. She turned out an endless supply of socks, sweaters and tapestries and presented them as gifts to some of her callers.

Suspicious, Pinkerton intercepted one of the female visitors and took a close look at her tapestry. It held a cunningly concealed message for the Confederates – a coded outline of the information Rose had gleaned from Fox.

Even Lincoln agreed now that a woman who could spy from behind bars was too dangerous a prisoner to keep.

In June 1862, Pinkerton escorted her to Fortress Monroe, where she signed a pledge 'not to return north of the Potomac' until the war was over. 'But then I shall return,' she assured him. 'And after we have burned your White House to the ground, I think we shall hang Old Abe in my yard to frighten away the crows.'

In fact, she was never to return.

Jefferson Davis, President of the Confederate States, sent her from his capital of Richmond to London in order to recruit money and sympathy for the Rebel cause. There she published a book of memoirs reviling Allan Pinkerton and detailing her affairs with Lincoln's traitorous friends. Suppressed in the United States, her book was an overnight sensation in England.

But on Rose's return voyage, the blockade runner carrying her was grounded on a shoal off the coast of Wilmington, North Carolina.

Too impatient to wait for rescue craft, Rose set out for shore in a small boat. The boat capsized in heavy seas, and her body was never found.

Double Deutsch
The Oxford University dons who turned up for a lecture by the
eminent psychologist Dr Emil Busch were puzzled but impressed.
The man they had come to see after answering an advertisement
in an Oxford newspaper had a flowing beard, a strong German
accent and a strange way of haranguing his audience so that most
of what he said was unintelligible. They later learned that 'Dr
Busch' was one of their undergraduates, and his entire speech had
been gibberish.

She left many questions behind her.

Never exposed during his lifetime, Harold Wilson went on to become a Vice-
President of the United States. Gustavus V. Fox escaped without a rebuke. And
though he knew their identities well, Lincoln took no action against any of the
traitors who had worked so intimately with Rebel Rose.

It may have been a fatal mistake. Historians agree that these same
conspirators could have been in league with John Wilkes Booth, the demented
actor who brought Lincoln's life to a violent end.

The general who died twice

What is the most difficult thing in the world to fake? Is it is signature?
A banknote, perhaps? Or an old master?

The answer must surely be: Your own death! Yet that is exactly
what an extraordinary military gentleman by the name of Michel Ney is
believed to have achieved in the winter of 1815.

Marshal Michel Ney was one of Napoleon Bonaparte's most able generals.
But after his army was defeated at Waterloo, Napoleon was exiled at St Helena –
and Ney, less lucky than his leader, was sentenced to death by firing squad.

Shortly after nine o'clock on the morning of December 7, Ney was led by a
contingent of the troops he had once commanded into the Luxembourg
Gardens in Paris. He was placed against a wall where he addressed his men in
the most emotional terms.

A British Diplomat witnessed the execution. He said that Ney shouted to the
firing squad: 'Comrades, when I place my hand upon my breast, fire at my

Marshal Michel Ney

heart.' The soldiers levelled their rifles, Ney put his hand to his chest, a volley rang out, and Ney fell, his coat stained with blood.

According to the observer, the body was then whisked away, with suspicious haste. It lay in a hospital overnight and was buried in the cemetery of Pierre la Chaise early the following day. Madame Ney did not attend the funeral. Only one distant relative was there to see the famous general laid to rest.

Three years later in Florence, South Carolina, a middle-aged French teacher using the name Peter Stuart Ney claimed that he and Marshal Ney were one and the same person. He said he had been saved from execution by a plot hatched by his old soldiers – with the aid of his former enemy, the British Duke of Wellington, who had been horrified by the ignoble fate proposed for a fellow general.

The teacher explained that the Paris firing squad had aimed above his head. He said that he had held in his hand a container of blood, which he had released when he struck his chest. He had then been smuggled by ship to America.

Nobody believed Peter Ney – until a doctor examined him and agreed that marks on his body conformed to Marshal Ney's battle scars. The teacher also claimed that during the passage to America he had been recognized by a fellow passenger – a soldier who had once been in his command. The man was later traced and confirmed the story. The French teacher also boasted a remarkably intimate knowledge of Marshal Ney and his family and of military tactics.

Then renowned New York handwriting expert David Carvalho examined letters written by the teacher and by the general. He had no hesitation in stating that they were written by the same person.

Six years after his Paris 'execution', one of Ney's pupils brought him a newspaper reporting the death of Napoleon on St Helena. The teacher fainted before his class and was carried home. Later that day he tried to cut his throat, but the knife broke in the wound.

Peter Ney – or Marshal Michel Ney – died peacefully in South Carolina in 1846. The last, weakly-spoken words of this frail old man were: 'I really am Marshal Ney'.

Chapter Seven

Imposters and Usurpers

'A face shaped by lotus petals, a voice as cool as
sandalwood, a heart like a pair of scissors, and
excessive humility; these are the signs of a rogue'
Sanskrit proverb

The Tichborne claimant

The largest and most ludicrous impostor of all time was an Australian cattle slaughterer from Wagga-Wagga named Arthur Orton – a corpulent con-man who became known through an amazing string of legal battles in the 1870s as 'The Tichborne Claimant'.

In March 1854 Sir Roger Charles Doughty Tichborne, a young British soldier and heir to a fortune, set off round the world to try to forget a disastrous love affair. He had fallen in love with his cousin, Katherine Doughty, but being Catholics, they could never wed.

Heartbroken, Tichborne resigned his commission in the Sixth Dragoon Guards and set sail in the small Liverpool sailing ship, the *Bella*, for South America. There his family hoped he would get over his romance.

After visiting Rio de Janeiro, the *Bella* headed north for New York – and was never seen again. Only the ship's log-book was found, floating 400 miles out to sea.

Roger's mother, Lady Tichborne, refused to accept the loss. She advertised in newspapers around the world for any information that could help locate her son. Shortly afterwards her husband died. In her grief she was more than ever convinced that Roger must still be alive. Then in 1866 came startling news – a letter from her son, supposedly dead for 12 years. She was overjoyed.

Unfortunately the Dowager Lady Tichborne was being hoodwinked by an altogether impossible claimant, cattle slaughterer Arthur Orton. Even at first glance he was an unlikely candidate. Sir Roger Tichborne had been a slight, sallow-faced man weighing barely nine stone. Arthur Orton was a ruddy-faced roly-poly 24-stone giant.

If Orton's appearance was dramatically different to young Tichborne's, so was his background. Orton was the youngest of 12 children of a poverty-stricken family living in the East End of London. He had gone to sea, deserted his ship in South America, returned briefly to England and, in 1852, emigrated to Australia.

Thirteen years later, deep in money troubles, he saw one of the Dowager Lady Tichborne's advertisements and, in a last desperate move to stave off bankruptcy, announced that he had estates in Britain.

After writing to the excited Lady Tichborne, hinting at a shipwreck, Orton raised several thousand pounds on the strength of his inheritance and sailed to Europe with his wife and baby daughter to meet the woman he hoped would become his mother. This dramatic meeting took place in Paris where the Dowager was then living. Orton insisted that the curtains be kept drawn – so this first encounter between son and mother took place in semi-darkness.

The impostor spoke to the old lady about his childhood. He mentioned meetings with his grandfather – who had died before Roger was born. He spoke of his old school, Winchester – whereas Roger had been educated at Stonyhurst. He alluded to his early Army service in the ranks – Roger had been a commissioned officer.

There were other discrepancies. Roger had a tattoo on his left arm. Orton had none. And Roger spoke fluent French. When his former French-language tutor questioned Orton, he found that the Wapping ex-seaman could not understand a word.

Yet the grief-stricken old lady who had lived so long in hope didn't care. She was convinced that Orton was her son. She explained away his errors of fact by saying: 'He confuses everything as in a dream.'

Orton could scarcely credit his luck. It didn't matter that no other members of the family believed him; he was sitting on a goldmine as long as the old lady lived. She immediately made him an allowance of £1,000 a year.

Orton now began to overstep the mark. Upon Sir Roger Tichborne's death, his younger brother Alfred had inherited the family estates. But he too had died young and Alfred's baby son, Henry, had taken the title. Orton now claimed his inheritance from Henry.

The case took over five years to prepare. Orton used the time to research the family history and even employed as servants two former members of Sir Roger's old regiment so that he could pick their brains about their former officer. Consequently no fewer than 30 of Roger's fellow-officers signed an affidavit that Orton and their dead comrade were one and the same person.

But just before the case opened, Orton lost his trump card. The Dowager Lady Tichborne died. So did her solicitor, who, strangely, had been one of Orton's most enthusiastic supporters. Undeterred, he proceeded.

The trial of the Tichborne Claimant opened on May 11, 1871. It continued for 103 days, during which time Orton produced over 100 witnesses prepared to state under oath that he was none other than Sir Roger Charles Doughty Tichborne. The family could muster only 17 witnesses to refute the claim.

Yet throughout the lengthy trial there were so many inconsistencies in Orton's story that although the old lady might have been fooled, a court of law was not deceived. The case collapsed and Orton was immediately arrested and charged with perjury. A new trial opened which lasted 188 days, ending on March 1, 1874, with Orton being sentenced to 14 years imprisonment.

The longest-ever British trial had spanned 1,025 days. Orton served 10 years and then had the nerve to return for another attempt on the Tichborne fortune. When this failed, he ended up exhibiting himself around the music halls. He died in a cheap lodging house on All Fools' Day, 1898.

Secret lives of military men

One of the most plausible impostors of all time was Dr James Barry. Noted for his dashing good looks, he joined the British army as a surgeon in 1816. He rose through the ranks to become the most skilled of physicians and later attained the exalted rank of Inspector General.

He showed conspicuous gallantry in campaigns around the world, even surviving a nasty wound in his thigh. He was greatly admired by his fellow officers. But the astonishing fact about our brave hero was that Dr James Barry was a woman.

No one knows who she really was. But it is recorded that in 1808, at the age of 13, she was accepted as a medical student at Edinburgh University in the name of James Barry. Fellow students said that she was somewhat nervous when walking out in rough neighbourhoods, that she refused to box and that she had the odd habit of keeping her arms folded over her chest.

But she wasn't a coward. In the army she became a noted duellist, and on one occasion after being insulted she gave a good account of herself with bare fists.

A fellow officer, however, did detect a certain 'effeminacy in his manner', and also praised 'his' conversation as being greatly superior to that usually heard at the mess table.

Only after Barry died was the dark secret discovered. To everyone's utter astonishment their Inspector General was revealed to be a woman. Even her own physician and her servant of 30 years were unaware of her true sex. But that wasn't the only shock. Further examination showed that Barry had been a mother.

The authorities were left with the perplexing question: why did this woman spend 53 years of her life as a man?

She is commemorated today in the Royal Army Medical College in Chelsea with a room called the Barry Room. It is the only part of the college where

---

Sex tale with no difference

Embarrassed police at Southend, Essex, could not be sure whether a long-haired suspect was male or female despite his (or her) assurances that he (or she) was a man.

They settled the problem by calling a police surgeon to find out whether he (or she) should be searched by a policeman or a policewoman. 'He' turned out to be a 'she'.

visiting ladies are permitted to remain unaccompanied.

An earlier case of a distinguished personage who chose to live in the guise of another sex was that of Chevalier D'Eon – a Frenchman who lived in the mid-18th century.

Being very feminine in looks, he took to swordsmanship to prove his masculinity. He became the greatest swordsman of his day and a highly successful French spy. Sent by Louis XV to spy on the Russian Court, the Chevalier dressed up as a woman, became lady-in-waiting to the Czarina and gathered much valuable information.

D'Eon's impersonations did not end with his spying days. He later came to London to the Court of St James as the French Ambassador. But because Louis XV had intimated that D'Eon was actually a woman, he turned up dressed as one, remaining in that guise for the rest of his life. Even so, many courtiers would lay bets as to whether the diplomat was really a man or woman.

Duelling and fencing at that time were learned and practised by most men in society. Despite his dress, the Chevalier became a fencing master of great renown and taught the aristocracy the fine art of duelling.

But this extraordinary man came to an even more extraordinary end. During a lesson he suffered a mortal wound when he fell on his opponent's sword – after tripping over his own skirts!

Thérèse and her priceless brick

Thérèse Humbert was the daughter of a French peasant, and she made a fortune out of a most audacious confidence trick. She drew inspiration from her father, who had lived his life in Toulouse on borrowed money raised against a vast inheritance – 'proof' of which he kept in an old sealed chest. When he died, his creditors called to claim the contents. They opened the chest and found a solitary house brick.

Like father like daughter, Thérèse fashioned a master-plan. She moved to Paris where she found a job as a washerwoman in the household of a government official. Here she deceived the boss's son into believing she was coming into money and he married her.

In due course, Thérèse had what appeared to be a fantastic windfall – a legacy of $20 million. She explained that it had been left her by Robert Henry

> **Taken for a ride**
> There was something the learner drivers did not know about their instructor – he had no licence himself. And the instructor used a stolen car for his lessons.
>   He was found out after driving a stolen car past a red traffic light and crashing into two other vehicles at Middlesborough, Yorkshire.
>   He was taken to court, where it was discovered that he ran a driving school and even branched out into coach-hire business – despite the fact that he had been banned from driving for 15 years.

Crawford, an American from Chicago. She had met him on a train two years previously and nursed him when he later suffered a heart attack.

The amazing story soon got around and when the young ex-washerwoman arrived at the bank, she received a warm welcome. She explained to the manager that Mr Crawford had actually left half of his fortune to be split between his two nephews in America and Thérèse's younger sister Marie. Out of the latter, Thérèse was to get an annual annuity but the full amount would not be realized until Marie reached the age of 21.

In addition, Thérèse explained, under the terms of the will and by agreement with the Crawford nephews, all the documents and deeds relating to the settlement were to be kept locked in her safe.

Thérèse told the manager: 'I am not allowed to open it until Marie comes of age, under penalty of forfeiting all claim upon the Crawford millions.' Then, predictably, she asked for a loan. It was readily granted.

The conniving trickster used the same ploy on several other banks. One Lille banker alone advanced her, over the years, seven million francs. And nobody ever questioned the contents of her safe – a massive contraption she kept hidden and locked in her splendid mansion bought with borrowed money.

Thérèse's position was now practically unchallenged . . . until the Lille banker, M. Delatte, happened to visit America. While there he tried to contact the Crawford family in Boston, where they were supposed to be living. Nobody in Boston or Chicago had ever heard of them or the deceased millionaire, Robert Henry Crawford.

The investigation proved disastrous not for Thérèse but for Delatte. His body was found floating in the East River in New York. The murderer was never caught.

With Marie's 21st birthday looming up, Thérèse now concocted a plan to make more crooked money, financing her brothers in a life insurance scheme that offered tempting returns. Instead of investing the incoming money, she spent it or paid off her more pressing creditors. Now she was 'La Grande Thérèse' and bankers and financiers pleaded with her to allow them to invest money in her schemes.

Then one high-ranking banker, Jules Bizat, decided to investigate. What he discovered shocked him – particularly as his own family had given the Humberts a small fortune – and he alerted the Prime Minister, Pierre Marie Waldeck-Rousseau.

The Premier decided against exposure but investors had to be warned. A series of scathing articles appeared in the influential newspaper *Le Matin*. Yet Thérèse's own lawyer believed so fervently in the truth of the Crawford inheritance that he threatened to sue the newspaper for libel and offered to open the safe to prove her virtue.

Thérèse, understandably, was horrified at this suggestion and covered up by protesting that such a procedure would dash all hopes of her getting her money. But the lawyer insisted that the safe should be opened to clear her name. Thérèse was trapped in the web of her own lies.

Two days before the safe was due to be opened, a mysterious fire broke out in Madame Humbert's apartment, totally gutting everything inside the room – except the safe. It was fireproof.

Some of France's leading financiers gathered around the safe on May 10, 1902. Thérèse was not present when the door was swung back to reveal . . . a brick!

Thérèse was later caught and sentenced to five years in prison. The safe, complete with brick, went on show in a Paris shop window, where it became one of the great tourist attractions of the year.

The 'count' from the backstreets of Sicily

For seven years, Count Cagliostro dazzled the high society of Europe's most fashionable cities. Royal courts marvelled as his magic elixirs performed apparent miracle cures. Scientists gasped at the gold and gems he could seemingly create from ordinary metal. Religious leaders believed him when he spoke of conversations with Moses and Solomon.

London, Paris and Strasbourg were bewitched by his glittering life-style.

Tales of his achievements spread like wildfire. A Baltic state offered him its throne. Ministers at the Tsar's Moscow court lined up relatives for him to heal.

Then, in France, he was thrown into the Bastille for a crime of which he was innocent. And shocked princes and priests learned that the count they had fêted was not what he seemed.

He was, in fact, a humble Sicilian named Giuseppe Balsamo. Born in a poverty-stricken back street of Palermo, in 1743, he had been living on his wits since stealing enough money from the church poor box and his uncle's savings to flee the island. He roamed the Mediterranean, staying for a while in Egypt, before settling to a lucrative life of crime in Rome, peddling home-made beauty creams and aphrodisiacs, copying paintings, forging banknotes and wills.

Here he met and married Lorenza Feliciani, a beautiful 15-year-old slum girl. Lorenza became the bait to lure rich victims into Balsamo's clutches. She was to help him reach the heights of fame and fortune – and send him tumbling to disgrace.

It was 1777 when the couple arrived in London. Rome had become too hot for them after a series of spectacular confidence tricks, and they had wandered for 10 years through southern Europe and North Africa, perfecting the art of deception. Now they were ready for the big time.

Overnight, Giuseppe and Lorenza Balsamo became Count Alessandrio di Cagliostro and Countess Serafina. He claimed he had stolen her from an Oriental harem. They lived up to their titles with the richest clothes and jewellery, elegant coaches and hordes of servants in sumptuous livery. When people asked where their money came from, admirers whispered that the Count had the power to turn base metals into gold.

The truth was more prosaic. The couple had arrived with £3,000, the proceeds of their Mediterranean adventures.

But shortly after arriving in London, Balsamo had joined a London lodge of Freemasons. Such Orders were spreading quickly throughout the Continent, with the richest, noblest men clamouring to join. Balsamo progressed quickly, being elected Grand Master of his lodge. And that opened many doors to him in Europe when he began travelling.

In Paris, he invented what he called an 'Egyptian Rite' order of Freemasonry, appointing himself head as Grand Cophta. This entitled him to collect heavy initiation fees and membership dues. And whereas Freemasonry was for men only, he opened a female lodge, with Lorenza in charge as the new Queen of Sheba.

Gullible Parisians flocked to join, lured by the promise of learning some of the Grand Cophta's secrets. The Queen of Sheba confided to duchesses that though she looked 30 – which she was – she was really 60. Her husband's magic five-drop potion kept her looking young.

Guiseppe and Lorenza Balsamo at their meeting with Comte de St. Germain

THE WORLD'S GREATEST CROOKS AND CONMEN

Listeners promised to keep her 'secret' – and became even more desperate to pay any price that the cure-all count demanded for his elixirs. His suave charm, irresistible bedside manner and touches of luxury – wrapping pills in gold leaf – all helped him get away with extortionate charges for herbal remedies any doctor could have prescribed.

As the Grand Cophta's fame spread, more and more countries demanded to see this man of magic powers for themselves. The nobles of the independent Baltic state of Courland were so impressed that they proposed crowning the count king. He wisely declined.

In Moscow one of the Tsar's ministers urged Cagliostro to cure his insane brother. The count deigned to inspect the patient, who was brought before him, securely bound. Acting on the count's instructions, the Russians untied the madman, and he charged his would-be benefactor, threatening to kill him. The count knocked him aside, then had him thrown into an icy river. Amazingly, when pulled out, the man was sane and apologetic.

But it was after he moved to Strasbourg in 1780 that Count Cagliostro achieved his greatest fame. By this time, he was claiming to have been born before Noah's flood, to have studied under Socrates, to have talked with Moses, Solomon and Roman emperors, to have drunk wine at a wedding feast in Cana, Galilee. And he was dating his letters 550 B.C.

He was also still confidently dispensing potions which cured patients whom ordinary doctors had given up as lost causes. The French government set up a commission of eminent medical men and scientists to investigate several unorthodox healers, and they pronounced many of Cagliostro's cures genuine, while admitting they could find no scientific explanation.

Soon his achievements came to the attention of the arrogant archbishop of the city, Prince-Cardinal Louis de Rohan. A servant was sent to summon Cagliostro – but returned alone with a message.

'If the prince is ill, let him come to me and I will cure him,' the count had said. 'If he is not ill, he has no need of me and I have no need of him.'

Such impudence was unheard of. But once de Rohan overcame his initial rage, he was intrigued enough to invent a minor ailment to justify visiting the man everyone was talking about. And so began the patronage that was to establish the count as one of Europe's most powerful men – and drag him down to despair.

When Cagliostro cured the Prince-Cardinal's brother, Prince de Soubise, of scarlatina – something the greatest doctors of Paris had failed to do – adulation knew no bounds. The count's effigy began appearing on snuff boxes, shoe buckles, rings and medallions.

Then de Rohan overstepped himself. Anxious to ingratiate himself with Queen Marie Antoinette, with whom he had fallen out of favour, he hatched a bizarre plot to obtain a diamond necklace she wanted. When King Louis XVI learned he had been forging letters in the queen's name and disguising a woman as the queen, he had the Prince-Cardinal arrested – and his protégés, the Cagliostros, were also thrown into the Bastille.

A public trial completely cleared them of involvement in the conspiracy, and nine months later they were escorted home in triumph by thousands of delighted supporters. But the damage had been done. Under intense interrogation. Lorenza had revealed too much about the tricks of Balsamo's trade. Slowly the truth about his money, his elixirs, his life-style began to emerge.

The furious Louis kicked the couple out of France, with dire warnings not to return. Again they wandered Europe, growing increasingly poor and shunned. Finally, Lorenza, tiring of her husband now that the glamour, riches and excitement had gone, persuaded him to return with her to Rome.

It was a crazy blunder – any Roman Catholic joining the Freemasons was subject to excommunication as a heretic. Yet Balsamo compounded his career by creating a new Egyptian Rite Masonic Lodge to try to revive his fortunes.

The papal police quickly seized him, and on April 7, 1791 he was found guilty of heresy and sentenced to die. Lorenza had denounced him, hoping to save herself. She was locked away in a convent for the rest of her life.

The Pope's mercy saved Balsamo for a while. The death sentence was commuted to life imprisonment in the dungeons of Italy's strongest fortress, San Leo. And there, on August 26, 1795, Count Alessandro di Cagliostro, the man who had proclaimed himself immortal, died, aged 52.

Is there a real doctor in the house?

The strange case of the queen and the bogus baron made the Dutch people look uneasily at their Head of State. For it was the second time that Queen Juliana of the Netherlands had been duped by a fraud 'psychiatrist'.

Her 'confessor' was really a Dutch labourer, Henry de Vries, 35. He shared a flat with the royal dressmaker, who introduced him to the queen as Baron David James Rothschild. The 69-year-old monarch took an instant liking to him and appointed him her psychiatrist.

Guards at the Soestdijk Palace, in The Hague, were so used to his frequent visits that they did not bother to check his papers. He was eventually exposed in 1978 when he applied for a police permit to hold a World Wildlife party in the grounds of the palace.

When the scandal broke, de Vries fled to France. Queen Juliana and her husband, Prince Bernhard, went on a long sea cruise in the late Aristotle Onassis's luxury yacht, *Christina*.

There were increasing fears at home that Juliana's powers of judgment were not all they should be. For she had been duped in the 1960s by another bogus 'psychiatrist', Greet Hoffman, whose powerful sway over her had caused a public outcry.

The former Dutch queen is just one of many victims of the age-old art of medical trickery – perhaps the greatest exponent of all being the resourceful impostor Ferdinand Demara.

Demara posed as a naval surgeon and saved many lives with his deft, self-taught surgery. He signed on the Royal Canadian Navy destroyer *Cayuga* during the Korean War when there was a desperate shortage of medical men.

The authorities accepted Demara's credentials, dispensing with the usual red tape, including fingerprint examination. His papers stated he was Dr Josephy Cyr, of New Brunswick. In fact, 30-year-old Demara had stolen them from Dr Cyr at a time when he was posing as a professor.

Once aboard the *Cayuga* as a surgeon-lieutenant, Demara's skills were called into immediate use: the captain needed a tooth extracted.

The bogus doctor sat up all night reading medical text books. Next morning he successfully removed the commander's tooth.

Sterner challenges soon followed. Nineteen badly wounded Korean civilians battled through the sea in a junk to beg for help from the *Cayuga*.

'I had to keep one basic principle in mind,' Demara recalled. 'The less cutting you do, the less patching up you have to do afterwards.'

The civilians responded well to the Canadian 'doctor's' skills. He had similar success with a South Korean soldier who was brought to him with a bullet near his heart.

Demara carried out cardiac surgery aboard ship as if he had been performing similar operations all his professional life. He later saved another soldier who had been smashed in the chest by a dum-dum bullet.

His downfall came when the Navy insisted on publicizing his heroic work. The real Dr Cyr read the story and an inquiry began. Investigations showed that, apart from posing as a doctor and a professor, Demara had also hoaxed his way across America disguised variously as a Trappist monk, a psychologist, a deputy sheriff, a prison warder and an instructor of theology.

He used forged references to get the jobs. Yet, once accepted, he invariably made a success of them. Indeed, had he not been so good a surgeon, he might still be conning his way through life – instead of reforming and settling down as a religious counsellor at a Californian hospital.

Young Barry Vinocur was praised for saving the life of an infant when he diagnosed a rare blood disease at the prestigious medical faculty of the University of California, San Francisco. He was so well regarded that he was deputed to lead a land and air emergency team for sick new-born babies.

Yet Vinocur was no doctor – he was a 33-year-old college drop-out with no formal medical training, who fast-talked his way into a job as a medical technician at a hospital in Cleveland, Ohio. Then he faked his physician's licence by using the medical records of his own cousin.

It was in Cleveland that Vinocur decided to create his false identity, after watching a real doctor vainly attempting to insert a catheter in the vein of a patient who was screaming in agony.

'I put on gloves and picked up the needle,' he said. 'I broke out in a cold sweat – and then put the needle in. It was then that I realized that I could do all these things myself.'

Vinocur's sham was uncovered in 1980, when a court put him on probation and ordered him to perform 100 hours of community service. The former 'doctor' was left with only one relic of his amazing days in the hospital wards: a textbook on intensive-care medicine which he had co-written with three real doctors.

Vinocur never made much money out of his good-natured duplicities. But Frank Abagnale – alias Dr Frank Williams – claimed to have been a millionaire twice over.

'I stole every nickel and blew most of it on gourmet food and luxurious living,' he said. 'But I never felt I was a criminal. I was simply a poseur and swindler of astonishing ability.'

His greatest coup came by chance after he had moved to Georgia in 1964, posing as Dr Frank Williams, a children's specialist. A neighbour was chief resident doctor at a nearby children's hospital, and invited 'Dr Williams' to look around.

Soon he was on the hospital staff – after reading every book he could find on children's diseases. If a term cropped up that he did not understand, Abagnale would surreptitiously consult a medical dictionary. But as a rule, when other doctors gave their diagnosis, he was only called on to nod agreement.

Eventually Abagnale realized his improbable role was putting young lives at risk and he resigned, having drawn a hefty salary for 11 months.

Next Frank Abagnale, alias Frank Williams, became 'Robert Conrad'. He put aside his medical text books and began studying borrowed law books, finally forging a degree for himself from Harvard Law School. He practised law for nine months before a colleague became suspicious.

Robert Conrad then became 'Frank Adams PhD, sociology teacher.' With fake documents he was hired by a Utah college as a teacher for three months.

Nobody was any the wiser. Said Abagnale: 'I just read a chapter ahead of the students and selected passages to emphasize.'

Then came a con-trick on a major American airline. Posing as a pilot, he got them to issue him with a uniform to replace his own 'stolen' one. With forged licence and identification as 'Captain Frank Williams' he flew as a standby co-pilot, with the crew on the flight deck.

But the con-man came down to earth with a bump in 1971. He was jailed for 12 years after admitting hundreds of charges. He was paroled four years later.

While in prison, Abagnale wrote a book on his life, aptly titled *Catch Me If You Can*, and came out a minor celebrity. He even appeared on the Johnny Carson TV show.

With his specialized knowledge, he started up businesses in Houston and Denver with an annual turnover of about $3 million. His speciality . . . crime prevention.

The 'professor' with an academic act

Thousands of former American college students owe their qualifications to the professor who never was. They were guided to examination success by a man who hoaxed his way into a series of top university posts – and proved he was suited for the job he had no right to hold.

Marvin Hewitt, born the son of a Philadelphia policeman in 1922, was a loner as a child. He discovered advanced mathematics at the age of 10, and was soon so well versed in the subject that neither his family nor his playmates could understand a word of what he was talking about.

He yearned to continue his studies at university, but could not qualify because routine schoolwork bored him. He left secondary school early, at 17, and for six years worked unhappily in factories and freight yards.

Then a newspaper advertisement caught his eye. A military academy needed a senior preparatory school teacher. Hewitt applied, claiming he was a Temple University graduate, and landed the post.

For the first time in his life he felt at home – admired and respected by pupils and fellow teachers alike. When the spring term finished, he decided to further his own education – as an aerodynamicist at an aircraft factory. He picked out a name from a universities' *Who's Who* list and landed a job on the strength of the borrowed qualifications. With his knowledge of advanced mathematics, even the most complex tasks were simple.

That summer, growing in confidence, he chose a fresh name for another post in education. Julius Ashkin was about Hewitt's age, had had a promising career at Columbia University and was about to start work as a teacher at the University of Rochester.

Hewitt usurped his name and qualifications, and applied to Philadelphia College of Pharmacy and Science for a job as physics teacher. He got it, at $1,750 a year. Students watched with admiration as their new master did complicated calculus in his head. And at the end of the year his classes did as well as any others in departmental examinations.

The only dark cloud on Hewitt's horizon was his salary. He felt Ashkin was entitled to better things. So he began writing to other colleges, enhancing his prospects by introducing the Christie Engineering Company in his list of references. This was a simple matter of getting letterheads printed, and hiring a secretarial service to handle mail.

Soon the Minnesota Bemidji State Teachers College sent Christie an inquiry about physicist Ashkin. They received a glowing testimonial – and Hewitt landed a job at $4,000 a year.

On the strength of his new-found means, Hewitt married. His wife Estelle was unperturbed by his bizarre explanation that because he had qualified under an assumed name he had to continue using it. She was even prepared to have all her 'Mrs Hewitt' mail delivered to a post-office box, and to put off her parents when they wanted to visit the couple.

Despite such precautions, Hewitt was running into problems. The president at Bemidji had also attended Columbia University, and was ever-ready to discuss mutual friends and acquaintances with 'Ashkin', a fellow campus old boy.

It was time to move on, and Hewitt decided to return to higher education, where he could mix with minds he considered more his equal.

Out came the Christie notepaper again, and back came an interview offer from the physics department at St Louis University. Hewitt was too scared to go, and wrote excusing himself, saying he could not get away on the suggested date. To his surprise, he was offered the post anyway, at $4,500 a year.

Now Hewitt was in his element. He was teaching graduate courses in nuclear physics, statistical mechanics and tensor analysis. He was proud of lecturing at Ph.D. level. Students liked him and fellow staff respected him, even if some did comment on inexplicable gaps in his knowledge of basic physics.

But again the close links between colleges and academics put his future in peril. A professor who travelled occasionally to Argonne National Laboratory, Chicago, for research, returned one day to tell Hewitt that he had run into an old friend who had worked with Ashkin at Columbia – and remembered him well.

Hewitt was now living on his nerves every time his colleague went to Chicago. But amazingly, the conversations at Argonne, faithfully reported on the professor's return, did not give the imposter away.

In the spring of 1948, Hewitt got another shock. An article appeared in the journal *Physical Review* – written by the real Julius Ashkin. Hewitt dashed to see his professor, and explained that he had written the paper, but signed it from Rochester University because that was where he had done the work on which it was based. Although his explanation was accepted, Hewitt wisely decided that there was a limit to how long his luck could last at St Louis.

He applied to the University of Utah at Salt Lake City, and received the red carpet treatment when he arrived for his interview. Glowing references from St Louis and Columbia backed up the good impression he made. Nobody realized that they were references for two different men. And nobody checked with Rochester University.

A dean at Columbia had even given Hewitt a quite unexpected 'insurance' bonus. He told Utah there had been two Ashkins on his books.

The Utah authorities were so delighted to get their man, they appointed him to a $5,800-a-year position as full professor. Hewitt had now overtaken the man whose qualifications he had borrowed. The real Ashkin was still an assistant professor at Rochester. It was the moment he had dreamed of. But his joy was not to last for long.

A month after he began work as head of department, a letter arrived addressed to 'Dr Julius Ashkin (?)'. It demanded that the masquerade be ended, but added:

'Let me assume that you are versed in theoretical physics and that you are a fundamentally decent man. I should then be willing to help you to relieve yourself of what must have become an almost unbearable burden. It is on these assumptions that I have decided not to take any immediate steps to notify university officials.'

The letter was from the real Julius Ashkin. And though he kept his word, one of his colleagues at Rochester was less merciful and tipped off the authorities. Hewitt was hauled before the Utah president and had to admit the truth. Generously, the authorities offered him the choice of staying on as a research fellow, to qualify for the degrees he needed to hold his position legitimately, or of transferring to another college to qualify.

But Hewitt was too shaken by events to take up either offer. He slunk back disgraced to his mother's home in Philadelphia, and for 18 months laid low, supported by his family and in-laws.

Then, in the spring of 1950, he launched a new bid for bogus academic fame. He wrote to a teachers' placement agency, announcing that George Hewitt, D.Sc., John Hopkins, was available for a posting. Qualifications included work as research director for the giant RCA communications company.

Hewitt had invented an RCA vice-president, and given him an address in Camden, New Jersey where letters could be sent – and answered by Hewitt.

The dead-letter ploy worked again. Hewitt took up an appointment teaching electrical engineering at Arkansas University's college of engineering, and flung himself into the work. Apart from lessons, he gave a local engineering society a lecture on 'The Orthogonality Property in Microwave Transmission.' He also presented a paper on 'The Theory of the Electron' at the Arkansas Academy of Science, and worked on two research programmes.

Then an RCA chief came to the university seeking engineering recruits. 'We have your former research director here,' he was told.

'Oh yes, who's that?'

'George Hewitt.'

'Who?'

It was back to Philadelphia for Hewitt. But by now he had twin baby sons to support as well as a wife. So he became Clifford Berry, Ph.D., Iowa State College, and took a post at New York State Maritime College.

Bored by teaching undergraduates, he tried to gatecrash technical industry. But this proved a tougher nut to crack than colleges. So he became Kenneth Yates, Ph.D., Ohio State University. And in January 1953 he began work teaching at the University of New Hampshire.

Again he was unmasked. One of his students in theoretical physics and relativity became suspicious of lapses in his tutor's knowledge. Checking a copy of the *American Men of Science* catalogue, he found the real Yates was working near Chicago for an oil company.

Confronted by the facts, Hewitt again owned up and quietly resigned. 'I always do all I can to straighten things out,' he said. But this time, any hopes he had of reappearing quickly in a new area were dashed. The news leaked to a newspaper, and quickly his career as a bogus boffin was splashed over every front page in the country.

Hewitt had always caused more trouble to himself than to anyone else. He said wistfully: 'If they'd only let me be a professor, I'd never want anything else or lie. I lied only to get those jobs. I was a good teacher, I've never really hurt anyone.'

The Princess from Javasu

One mild April evening in 1817 near the village of Almondsbury in Gloucestershire, a mysterious beautiful girl appeared. She was aged about 20, was penniless, lost and bewildered and spoke a tongue that no-one had ever heard before.

It was obvious she was in need of food and shelter, and a kindly magistrate, Mr. Worral, took pity on her and invited her into his house. There he and his wife tried to illicit some information from her about where she'd come from and who she was. But all the girl would say was 'Caraboo!' Over and over again: 'Caraboo! Caraboo!' Mr and Mrs Worral asked in sign language if that was her name. She nodded.

At least that was established. But not much else was forthcoming. She seemed to get excited by an oriental picture, would only eat food if she prepared it herself in a special way, and she insisted on sleeping on the floor.

As luck would have it, after a few weeks a Portuguese appeared on the scene – Signor Manuel Eynesso, who had spent some time in the Far East. He was called round to meet Caraboo and after a short time alone with her, announced he could understand every word she spoke.

This truly amazed everyone, including Caraboo – since she didn't understand what she said herself.

According to the Portuguese 'interpreter', Miss Caraboo was a princess in her country, an island near Sumatra called Javasu. After a war in which the Boogos, or cannibals, killed her mother, she was kidnapped by Malay pirates who sold her into slavery. She was bought by a ship's captain whose vessel visited a southern African port and then continued on to Europe to an unknown destination. Princess Caraboo escaped her master while the ship sheltered from a storm and she swam ashore. She wandered round the countryside for many weeks before finding refuge in the village.

Signor Eynesso's sensational disclosures amazed the whole country. More experts came from all over the examine the mysterious princess. And she certainly didn't let them down. She performed wild dervish-like dances, twirling around holding one leg in the air. She confused the greatest linguists with her strange tongue. And she drew up characters of the 'Javasu' language.

Yet all this was an elaborate fraud and imposture . . . by a cobbler's daughter from Devon called Mary Baker. She had dreamed up the act to get into a wealthy household and escape from her impoverished and boring environment.

The Portuguese, Eynesso, had been an added bonus and when they were alone Mary had somehow persuaded him to join in the deception.

Princess Caraboo

But Mary's fame as Princess Caraboo soon led to her downfall. A Bristol woman named Mrs Neale read an account of Caraboo. The description of the princess was identical to a girl who, Mrs Neale claimed, lodged with her for several weeks. A meeting between Mrs Neale and Caraboo was arranged.

Mrs Neale immediately recognised Mary and exposed her. The girl confessed. But with her background of family poverty, desertion by her parents and near starvation, everybody took pity on poor Mary. She was given the passage money to go off to America to make a new life.

America didn't work out either for this exotic adventuress. Seven years later she was back in Bristol trying to exhibit herself as Princess Caraboo for a shilling a peep. But she wasn't successful, and she ended her days selling leaches to people who wished to avoid physician's bills by bleeding themselves.

The saved exotic

Another imposter supposedly from far-off shores was a remarkable man who called himself George Psalmanazar. In 1703 he arrived in London claiming to be from Formosa, a country about which little was known at the time. He also claimed to have been converted to Christianity and sponsored by the Bishop of London as an important convert. He was immediately lionized by London society, including Dr Johnson, as 'a saved exotic'.

Doted on by the famous, he was given chambers and asked to translate the Bible into his native tongue. He couldn't, of course, although he burned candles at his window all night to convince people he was working on the project. But he did invent a Formosan language, lectured on the country and offered to teach the language to future missionaries. And in 1704 he wrote an Historical and Geographical Description of Formosa.

As was the 'custom' in Formosa, he only ate raw meat and he astonished Londoners with tales of the annual sacrifice of 18,000 infants to the pagan Formosan gods. He claimed the average life expectancy was 100 years, guaranteed by a regular diet of snakes' blood for breakfast.

This was an age when average life expectancy was a meagre 40 years and people's diet basically consisted of meat and potatoes. Obviously, a life-span of 100 years would have been unheard of.

He also strongly advocated a daily dip. Again, this astounded people. Londoners bathed very seldom and preferred to use scent to disguise bodily smells. However, it is debatable whether he practised what he preached.

Then a strange thing happened to George. Impressed by the kindness and generosity of Londoners, he really was converted to Christianity. He repented, confessed everything, was forgiven – and lived out the rest of his days like a saint. But the two things he never revealed were where he actually came from and who he really was.

Chapter
Eight

Pranksters and Hoaxers

'Life is a joke that's just begun'
Sir W.S. Gilbert

The Piltdown 'missing link'

In 1912 two men made monkeys out of the world's scientific establishment. One of them was a quiet, studious English country lawyer and respected amateur geologist named Charles Dawson. But it is the name of the other that has gone down in history – Piltdown Man.

Piltdown Man was the title given to a prehistoric humanoid skull which Dawson claimed to have discovered in a gravel pit near Piltdown Common, Sussex. He had been tipped off about bones in the pit by a workman. Dawson had spent many days searching the pit. First he turned up a few tiny fossilized bone fragments. Then he found flint tools, fossilized teeth – and finally parts of a skull.

The lawyer packaged up his treasures and sent them to an acquaintance, one of the world's leading authorities on the history of man, palaeontologist Dr Arthur Smith Woodward of the British Museum.

Woodward was so excited that, at the first opportunity, he sped down to Sussex to join Dawson at the gravel pit. His enthusiasm knew no bounds, for here at last was the discovery that scientists had anxiously awaited for half a century – the proof of Charles Darwin's controversial Theory of Evolution.

When Darwin published his *Origin of Species* in 1859, he was denounced as a crank and even a heretic. Even the more level-headed critics demanded to be shown some proof of his theory. Where, they asked, was the Missing Link? Why had no one ever discovered any fossilized remains of the creatures that Darwin claimed linked man with the ape? Here thought Woodward, was that proof.

He and Dawson carefully sifted through the gravel pit debris in the area where the first bones had been unearthed. More finds were made and other experts called in. They agreed – Piltdown Man was indeed the Missing Link.

They pointed to the thick bone structure of the skull fragments, to the tiny brain area, to the ape-like jaw – and, above all, to the teeth which were ground down, not in the manner of an ape, but as human teeth are worn away.

Woodward painstakingly pieced together the finds until they formed the greater part of a complete skull – and announced that what they had unearthed was a creature, half-man half-ape, which had lived 500,000 years ago. Although the skull was that of a woman, the find was officially named *Eoanthropus dawsoni* – Dawson's Early Man.

The announcement threw scholars worldwide into dizzy delight. Piltdown was scheduled to be named a National Monument. Dawson became a hero. Woodward wrote a book about this discoverer of 'the earliest Englishman'. The British Museum displayed the skull with a pride bordering on rapture.

Even the local public house changed its name to The Piltdown Man.

Mr Charles Dawson and Dr A Smith Woodward

Trippers travelled by the coachload to view the site of this earth-shattering find.

Dawson continued his excavations in the Piltdown area and, over the next few years, pieced together parts of a second skull. The finds only ended when he died in 1916, at the age of 52. Others continued the search but no further evidence was ever found.

The drying-up of the discoveries after Dawson's death was realized later to have been no coincidence. For Piltdown Man was a fake.

The skull was indeed that of a human, but the jaw and teeth were those of an orang-utan. The teeth had been filed down to look like human teeth, then the skull had been skilfully stained and aged before being broken up and buried in the gravel pit.

Right from the start, a few sceptics had raised doubts about the authenticity of Piltdown Man. But the cynics were not allowed access to the relics to make more thorough tests. All requests to have the samples scraped and probed were turned down. It was not until 1949 that one of Woodward's successors at the British Museum, a young geologist, Dr Kenneth Oakley, was allowed to take samples of the skull fragments and subject them to chemical tests. His verdict: the skull was not 500,000 years old but 'only' 50,000 years old.

Oakley, too, was wrong. In 1953, using newly developed techniques of age assessment, more extensive tests were made by a committee of paleontologists.

They finally and officially declared Piltdown Man a fake.

Who had perpetrated such an elaborate and outrageous confidence trick at the expense of the scientific world?

Although nobody was ever able to prove it, Hoax Suspect Number One has always been Charles Dawson. He had never sought money on the strength of his 'discovery'. But he was ambitious for academic distinction. And once a visitor had once walked into his laboratory uninvited to find Dawson busy over a bubbling crucible – staining bones.

The other prime suspect was Australian-born Sir Grafton Elliot Smith, one of the leading experts then employed by the British Museum. He had the temperament for such a massive practical joke. His possible motive: to liven up the deathly atmosphere pervading the famous mausoleum.

Whoever the culprit was, he took his secret with him to the grave – and left behind some very red scholarly faces.

The gigantic hoax

George Hull pulled off a giant of a fraud – literally. The cigar-maker from Binghampton, New York, decided to line his pockets with a scheme that was big in every way.

In 1868 Hull read about a race of giants that were supposed to have inhabited the earth. Anyone who discovered the remains would be on to a fortune, he thought. People would pay dearly to see such a giant.

So Hull set about 'making' his own giant. He bought a massive block of gypsum from a quarry in Iowa and sent it secretly to Chicago to be carved into a 10-ft-high naked giant.

Thanks Pal

Report in a Sussex newspaper:
'Mr Michael Vanner, of Bexhill Road, St Leonards, a defendant in a recent case at Hastings Magistrates' Court, wishes to state that Mr Melvin Peck, whom he pleaded not guilty to assaulting, was not a passer-by, as stated, but is a friend of his.'

When it was complete the stone was treated with chemicals to make it look as though it had been buried beneath the earth for millions of years. Then, unknown to his cousin William Newell, he buried the stone giant on Newell's farm in New York State.

Hull bided his time. With a bit of gentle persuasion he got Newell to start drilling for water on the farm. Wells were sunk all over the farm and in October 1869 the 'giant' was discovered.

Newell was overjoyed. He bought a tent, erected it over the find and charged the public 50 cents to see the marvel. The news that some genuine fossilized bones had been found close by added to the attraction.

It was now time for Hull to make his move. He returned to his cousin's farm and persuaded him to increase the admission price to one dollar. He even got Newell to read a lecture on the giant which he had specially written.

The crowds flocked by coach and train to see what Newell termed the Eighth Wonder of The World. Experts were also taken in until one, Oliver Wendell Holmes. bored a hole in the skull and found it was solid.

But the public were not put off. They still turned up in their thousands to see the giant.

The end came when a private investigator traced the connection between Hull and Newell and got on the trail of the block of gypsum. The game was up. Hull confessed to his con and renamed the giant Old Hoaxey. It still exists today, resting in the New York State Farmer's Museum.

It has been estimated that Hull and Newell picked up about £55,000 from their giant swindle.

'Princes' who fooled the navy

While the officers and men of the *Dreadnought* prepared for their VIP visitors, an elegant man in top hat and morning coat was introducing himself to the stationmaster at London's Paddington Station. He announced himself as Herbert Cholmondesly of the Foreign Office and he demanded a special train to be laid on immediately to convey a party of Abyssinian princes to Weymouth.

Cholmondesly was none other than William Horace de Vere Cole. It was he who had sent a telegram and it was he who had recruited five of his friends to perpetrate one of the most imaginative and elaborate hoaxes of all time.

The four princes who boarded the special train at Paddington on February 7 were really Cole's accomplices in this amazing confidence trick. All had been heavily made up, bearded and robed by theatrical make-up expert Willy Clarkson. It was his best day's work.

Clarkson watched proudly as the Abyssinian potentates were ushered into a specially prepared carriage. Beneath the elaborate disguises were famous novelist Virginia Woolf, sportsman Anthony Buxton, artist Duncan Grant and judge's son Guy Ridley. Accompanying them as an 'interpreter' was Virginia Woolf's brother Adrian. And bringing up the rear the 'man from the FO', Cole himself.

The group's reception at Weymouth was better than the hoaxers had ever dreamed of. A red carpet stretched from the train down the platform and through the station concourse. Waiting beyond was a guard of honour which they graciously inspected.

The party was taken by launch to the *Dreadnought* which had been bedecked with bunting for the royal visit. They were ceremoniously piped aboard.

The princes were invited to inspect the mighty ship. As they wandered around they handed out visiting cards printed in Swahili and spoke Latin in a strange accent. 'Bunga-bunga,' they exclaimed whenever they were shown some awesome aspect of the warship.

They overacted their roles to a ludicrous degree. They asked for prayer mats at sunset and they even tried to bestow Abyssinian honours on some of the senior officers.

On three occasions they almost gave the game away. The royal guests were offered a princely repast aboard the *Dreadnought*; they declined and Cole had to explain that their religious customs precluded them from eating or drinking at sea. The real reason for their refusal, however, was a warning by make-up man Clarkson that if they tried to eat anything, their false lips would fall off!

Later the hoaxers' hearts sank as they were introduced to an officer who was related to Virginia Woolf and who had met Cole on several occasions. The officer looked both of them square in the face yet failed to recognize either.

The third moment of panic occurred when Anthony Buxton sneezed and one half of his moustache flew off but he stuck it back again before anyone noticed.

The visit ended with Press photographs and an uproarious journey back to London during which the tricksters laughed themselves hoarse. The Royal Navy hierarchy were left congratulating themselves as being paragons of protocol – while Cole congratulated his phoney princes on the hoax of the decade.

The entire operation had cost Cole £4,000. But he counted it money well spent in his one-man campaign to bring the posturing and the pompous down a peg or two.

Oh come, all ye trustful!

Theodore Hook was a poet and wit who lived nearly 200 years ago in Regency London. Hook's hoaxes began gently enough – they were more in the nature of fun and japes – but his most ambitious one involved hundreds of London celebrities, including royalty.

Once at the Drury Lane Theatre he hid under the stage during the performance of a tragedy. When the leading actor began his crucial soliloquy, Hook accompanied him with a tune on a penny whistle. The stage was also the scene for another of Hook's pranks. He walked on in the middle of a performance and delivered a joke letter to the leading man telling him he had inherited a fortune. The actor apologized to the audience, jubilantly announced his good luck – and walked off stage, bringing the performance to a close.

Hook didn't become too popular with theatregoers. But he has to be remembered for one of the greatest hoaxes in history. It took place on November 10, 1810, as the result of this wager he made with a friend:

'I wager I can make an ordinary house in an ordinary street – how about this one, for example, No 54 Berners Street – the most famous address in the whole of London.'

His friend, obviously thinking he was on to a good thing, eagerly accepted the bet.

Over the next few days Hook began writing letters to hundreds of people. Then on November 10, Theodore Hook and his friend rented a room in the house opposite No. 54, a shabby, nondescript little dwelling occupied by a widow named Mrs Tottenham.

At precisely 9.0 am the first of many callers arrived. It was the coalman, with several sacks of coal that had never been ordered. Then came the fishmonger, the florist, the butcher and the cabinetmaker.

Hook had written to all these merchants and many more asking them to come to No. 54 Berners Street at the appointed hour on November 10. There were chimney sweeps, undertakers, doctors and dentists, cabs, carriages and carts.

Under various absolutely credible pretexts, Hook had invited not just tradesmen and merchants, fashionable medics and professionals to the house, but also really important personages. With hundreds of people pouring into Berners Street, Hook happily watched the resulting confusion. But his greatest triumphs were yet to come.

The Governor of the Bank of England arrived – to keep an appointment with a criminal who was to reveal inside information on a major counterfeiting

Theodore Edward Hook

fraud. The Archbishop of Canterbury turned up – to collect a large bequest for the Church of England. Then came the Lord Mayor – to collect a special philanthropic donation on behalf of the City of London. The Lord Chief Justice, too, came and went. And the Lord Chancellor.

The day was crowned with the arrival of a detachment of guards, the chief of police and none other than the Duke of York, who was son of the King of England and Commander-in-Chief of the British Army.

Hook had, without doubt, won his wager. London was brought to a standstill, as traders, merchants, diplomats and the hoi-polloi struggled to make their way to and from Berners Street. But at that time, of course, only two people knew who was behind the scheme. The secret cost Hook's friend £1,000. Hook discreetly left the country.

'Poor old prospectors' struck pure gold!'

On a summer day in 1872, two grizzled prospectors, Philip Arnold and John Slack, ambled into the Bank of California in San Francisco. They had with them a drawstring sack, which they cautiously handed to the teller.

'How about keeping this for us,' Slack drawled, 'while me'n him go and get drunk?'

The teller agreed, but as soon as the prospectors had left the bank he peeked at the contents of the pouch. Then he rushed into the office of his boss, the financial czar William Ralston, a man whose greed matched his girth. Expecting to see a few pinches of gold dust, Ralston opened the sack. A cataract of living fire spilled across his desk – a fortune in uncut diamonds.

At the end of a feverish three-day search, Ralston found the missing prospectors in a saloon. But even after he'd sobered them up they proved tough customers.

Grudgingly they admitted to having found a diamond field 'bigger than Kimberley'. But they said they hadn't acquired title to the land and refused to tell him where it was located. Much as they would appreciate Ralston's financial backing, anyone who inspected their find must agree to make the entire journey blindfold.

Ralston agreed, sending his mining engineer David Colton. The man returned in three weeks, wild with excitement. It was all true, Colton said, displaying his own find – a fistful of diamonds.

Ralston paid the two miners $50,000, put another $300,000 aside for their use, and promised them an additional $350,000 when their project started producing. Others who contributed money included Baron Anthony de Rothschild, the editor Horace Greeley, General George B. McClellan, and Charles Lewis Tiffany, founder of the world's greatest jewellery business.

To pull in still more smart money, Ralston sent another inspection party to the field. Again, they were led by Arnold and Slack. The visitors travelled by rail to Rawlings, Wyoming, where the prospectors blindfolded them and took them on a long trek through wild rangeland.

When the blindfolds were lifted, the view stunned them. Ant hills in the valley shimmered with diamond dust. More than that, there were rubies scattered across the terrain like plums in a pudding.

When the party returned home with their astonishing report, Ralston's avarice knew no bounds. His first step was to dump the two old-timers.

The game, he told them, was far too rich for their blood. Bullying them with threats of strange legal manoeuvres, he persuaded his grizzled victims to accept $700,000 for their share. Apparently hoodwinked by a great robber baron, they took the money and ran.

By now the diamond lode was a worldwide sensation, but eminent geologist E. W. Emmonds doubted the whole story – he had seen no signs of diamonds anywhere in Wyoming.

Doubling back on his trail, he located the great discovery. He was immediately alerted by the fact that the site lay only a few miles from the rail-line. The blindfolded members of Ralston's party had simply been led round in circles. Then he found that the 'ant hills' were man-made and there was something very strange about all the diamonds. The first one he picked up showed the marks of a lapidary tool. Emmons wired the bad news to San Francisco. The field had been 'salted'.

It hit the money marts with bombshell force, and by nightfall Ralston's diamond syndicate had become a joke.

It was revealed that the prospectors had visited Europe before setting up the con-trick, covering their tracks by sailing from and returning through Halifax, Nova Scotia. In Europe they had spent $35,000 – their life savings – on the gems they scattered across Wyoming soil.

Public sympathy was with the hoaxers, and they were never prosecuted. Slack later drifted away to parts unknown, Arnold to Kentucky, where he founded his own bank. But it did little better than that of William Ralston, whose great institution collapsed in 1875.

The dismantling of Manhattan Island

The 19th century was not a golden age for America. Two wars and several economic depressions left little to laugh about. Yet, possibly because of these traumas, it seems to have been a boom time for hoaxers. No hoax can have been more ridiculous than the project dreamed up by two tricksters in 1824 to slice off Manhattan Island and put it back again the other way round! Yet, incredibly, many people believed them.

It was claimed that Mayor Stephen Allen was seriously worried about the Battery, the island's southern end, where many new buildings had been erected. It was starting to sag dangerously under the weight, and could sink at any moment with great loss of life and property.

The plan was to amputate the Island at the Kingsbridge or northern end. It would then be floated down past Ellis Island, turned round and moored in a safer position.

Cautious at first, hundreds of workmen and contractors were later completely sold on the idea. They swarmed into the parnters' plush office to get in on the historic project.

In the next eight weeks, the pair collected an array of mammoth saws 100 ft long with 3-ft teeth. Even paying some salaries in advance, they hired 300 labourers to do the sawing.

They also found two dozen oars 250 ft long and signed up another 2,000 men to row the island across the bay. Gigantic anchors were leased to hold the island firm in case of a storm.

Second-hand surgery

Francis Murphy amputated a toe and undertook complicated hip surgery on an elderly woman during 17 successful operations at Redhill General Hospital, southern England. And it was not until after he was sacked – for a row with a senior consultant – that the hospital discovered he was a phoney who had learned his techniques from his medical student wife. Murphy, who had conned other hospitals in England, Canada and Ireland, was jailed for two years.

Edgar Allan Poe

On the big day, dozens of greedy contractors, hundreds of workmen and thousands of sightseers turned up to launch the project. Also there was Mayor Allen, who was simply trying to find out what on earth was going on. The only people not around were the two promoters of the project. They were never seen again.

Another great hoax of the age was perpetrated by a newspaper that tried to make its own news. Desperate to increase its readership, the *New York Sun* ran stories of an amazing telescope with a huge lens that magnified objects 42,000 times. According to the reports, the telescope showed that there was life on the Moon, including a strange ball-like creature that rolled at great speeds. During these sensational reports, the paper's circulation rose from 2,500 to 19,000.

Another great newspaper hoax was author Edgar Allan Poe's account of a transatlantic crossing by balloon. Millions of readers eagerly awaited for Poe's reports – which the famed horror-story writer made up from start to finish.

Then there was the 'Terrible Turk' – not a person but supposedly a chess-playing robot that drew huge audiences. This bizarre-looking contraption took on all-comers and made strange machine sounds as it played. It took years – and lots of money for its owner, Johann Maelzel – before someone found that the real chess genius was a dwarf hidden inside the 'Terrible Turk'.

Who do you think you're kidding?

Hoaxers come in all shapes and sizes – and a multitude of disguises. Some perpetrate their cunning uses for money, others – like the honest hoaxers in this final chapter – carry out their con-tricks just for the joy of making a lot of suckers look silly!

But only one man has ever been able to hit the hoaxers' highspot – a fake entry in the American edition of *Who's Who*. That man was Professor Rutherford Aris, a noted chemical engineer who was already listed in the book. But when the *Who's Who* compilers wrote asking him to fill in any further biographical details, they incorrectly addressed the letter to 'Aris Rutherford'.

Professor Aris wrote back with details of a completely new fictional character whose birthplace was a Scotch whisky distillery, whose job was as a whisky consultant, and whose hobby was drinking the stuff. *Who's Who* printed the lot.

One of America's most persistent pranksters was humourist Edgard Nye.

Alan Abel, international hoaxer –

PRANKSTERS AND HOAXERS

Once, when travelling by train with poet James Whitcomb Riley, he spotted a ticket inspector approaching. Nye, who had been looking after the tickets, said to his friend: 'I've lost one of them. Quick, get under the seat'.

The poet complained but obeyed. However, when the inspector arrived at their seats, Nye handed to him, not one, but both tickets. 'Who is the other ticket for?' asked the inspector. 'For my friend,' said Nye, pointing under the seat with one hand, while tapping his temple knowingly with the other.

More recently, another American joker, comedian Alan Abel, played a trick on the entire nation. He formed the Society Against Indecency of Naked Animals to persuade owners to dress their dogs, cows and other animals in special underwear to preserve the creatures' modesty. It was meant to be a joke but the Press and public took the whole idea seriously.

At the height of the Vietnam War, President Lyndon Johnson asked if he could visit an air-base to cheer up some of the boys who were about to be drafted to south-east Asia. The visit was duly arranged. But by the time the President turned up, the troops who were on their way to war had tried to drown their sorrows to such an extent that they were deemed unfit to be paraded before him.

Then one of the Army's public relations men had a brainwave. Instead of using the outgoing troops, another batch of young men were introduced to Johnson. They were a laughing, joking, hand-shaking squad whose morale was at an all-time high – because they had just come *back* from Vietnam.

President Johnson was most impressed: so much so that he extended his visit to be able to wave the soldiers goodbye. Which meant the Army having to put their homecoming troops straight back into a plane and flying them round in circles until Johnson had left the base.

One hoax which is known to be pure fiction is the novel of Penelope Ashe. Miss Ashe appeared to have one of the sure-fire American best-sellers of the 1970s with her book, *Naked Came the Stranger*, a story of sex in suburbia. In just three days, 20,000 copies were sold, paperback rights were bought and 18 film companies made inquiries. It even got a write-up in the prestigious *New York Times Book Review*.

But at the end of the week, publishers and agents began to worry because all their attempts to track down Penelope Ashe were hitting dead-ends. That's when New York newspaper columnist Mike McGrady announced: 'The book is a hoax.'

McGrady had invented Miss Ashe so that he could produce his idea of a really abysmal novel. He recruited 24 co-authors, and they polished off the whole book, a chapter each, in just three weeks. None of them had expected the novel to be quite as successful as it turned out.

Another literary hoaxer was Cyril Henry Hoskins. Clever make-up helped him pull off a remarkable con-trick.

Hoskins wrote a string of money-spinning books about his life in a non-existent Tibetan monastery. He called himself Lama Lobsang Rampa, and claimed that a hole had been drilled in his shaven head to accommodate a spiritual 'third eye'.

Thousands of people thought there was magic in the air one morning when astronomer Patrick Moore told radio listeners tuned to the British Broadcasting Corporation that at exactly 9.47 am the planet Pluto would pass behind Jupiter, producing an increased gravitational pull from the heavens.

Moore said that when that happened people would feel lighter, and he invited them to jump into the air to experience a floating sensation. That was how thousands of people across Britain came to be leaping into the air at 9.47 am on April 1, 1976 – April Fools' Day. Hundreds of listeners actually rang the BBC afterwards to say that the experiment had worked!

Famous BBC broadcaster Richard Dimbleby fooled the nation nine years earlier – on April 1, 1957 – when he showed a television documentary about the spaghetti harvest in Italy. Viewers saw the spaghetti wafting in the wind as it 'grew' from the branches of trees. Because he was such a distinguished broadcaster, thousands believed him.

One radio station had a hoax played on it when it invited a VIP visitor, His Serene Highness Prince Shubtill of Sharjah, to be interviewed about oil exploration in the Persian Gulf. The interview was recorded for a news bulletin on Liverpool's Radio City, and the prince left after being fêted by the management.

But his Serene Highness was prankster Neville Duncan, a bank computer expert . . . and his impersonation was discovered 20 minutes too late when interviewer Peter Gould, a crossword fanatic, realized that Prince Shubtill's name was not Arabian after all, but an anagram for Anglo-Saxon bull****.

There was panic in 1977 when an unknown electronics wizard broke into a peak-hour national newscast on British television and announced that beings from outer space had landed in Southern England. TV station and newspaper switchboards were jammed, but the hoaxer was never discovered.

But creatures from outer space are small fry compared to the giant monster of Loch Ness. Sightings of the famous 'Nessie' have been reported for more than 1,000 years, but in 1972, experts believed they had at last captured the 'beastie'.

What they did not know was that, some weeks earlier, the crew of a British cargo vessel taking live elephant seals from the Falkland Islands to a zoo in England had found one of the seals dead. They threw the body overboard and it was picked up in the nets of a fishing boat. For a prank, the fishermen dumped the body in Loch Ness.

It was found there by zoologists organizing a large-scale search for the monster. The experts packed the half-ton, 15-ft giant in ice, loaded it into a van

Richard Dimbleby

and headed south for England to announce their news to the world.

However, locals alerted the police to the monster-snatchers' activities and the order was flashed to all cars: 'Nessie must not leave Scotland – she belongs to us'. Roadblocks were set up and the van was eventually stopped on the Forth Road Bridge. The phoney Nessie was impounded by police. Its true identity was revealed only after a blaze of publicity.

Money, purely and simply, was the aim of the Trodmore Hoaxers, a gang who invented a complete Cornish town, which they called Trodmore. But the only piece of fictitious real estate in which they were interested was the racecourse.

Just before a Bank Holiday, one of the gang, calling himself 'Mr Martin of St Ives' delivered to the editor of *The Sportsman* a racecard for Trodmore. It duly appeared in the paper. None of the horses ever ran, but the 'winner' was later announced. It was a horse called Reaper, and the gang had placed dozens of bets on it with bookmakers throughout London. They got their money and were never caught.

Another sporting hoax – for fun, this time, not money – was perpetrated on the organizers of the 1976 British Open golf tournament. One of the contestants who was accepted for the tournament was Mr Maurice G. Flitcroft, a Barrow-in-Furness shipyard worker who had never even tried to play a full 18 holes of golf in his life. But, as his professional partners stamped and fumed, the cheeky Mr Flitcroft managed to blunder round the course – in 121 shots!

Hot pants

A 30-year-old Lebanese businessman flew to Copenhagen airport to pick up four sample pairs of jeans for his brother's clothing company. But when he opened the package he got a shock – it contained £120,000 in different currencies. The money belonged to a London company.

The Lebanese stared into the parcel, then made up his mind. He picked up the bag, returned to the airport and bought a ticket to Athens via Frankfurt. Then he disappeared, leaving his wife and three children back in Copenhagen.

Said the deserted wife: I can't blame him. He did the right thing.'

PDO 83-1083